MISSOURI
CAVES
IN HISTORY
AND LEGEND

PROJECT SPONSORS

Missouri Center for the Book
Western Historical Manuscript Collection
    University of Missouri–Columbia

SPECIAL THANKS
Christine Montgomery, State Historical Society of Missouri,
    Columbia
Judy Holmes, Lyons Memorial Library, College of the Ozarks

MISSOURI HERITAGE READERS
General Editor, Rebecca B. Schroeder

Each Missouri Heritage Reader explores a particular aspect of the state's rich cultural heritage. Focusing on people, places, historical events, and the details of daily life, these books illustrate the ways in which people from all parts of the world contributed to the development of the state and the region. The books incorporate documentary and oral history, folklore, and informal literature in a way that makes these resources accessible to all Missourians.

Intended primarily for adult new readers, these books will also be invaluable to readers of all ages interested in the cultural and social history of Missouri.

OTHER BOOKS IN THE SERIES

MISSOURI CAVES IN HISTORY AND LEGEND

H. Dwight Weaver

University of Missouri Press
Columbia and London

Library of Congress Cataloging-in-Publication Data

Weaver, H. Dwight.
  Missouri caves in history and legend / H. Dwight Weaver.
    p. cm.
  Summary: "Examines the historical and cultural significance of Missouri caves,
describing ways that people have used them historically for shelter, cold storage,
burials, moonshine stills, mining, and even as hideouts for Civil War soldiers and
outlaws including Jesse James. Describes growing public appreciation and conservation of these unique and beautiful resources"—Provided by publisher.
  Includes index.
  ISBN 978-0-8262-1778-3 (alk. paper)
  1. Caves—Missouri—History. 2. Speleology—Missouri. 3. Caves—Social
aspects—Missouri—History. 4. Missouri—History, Local. 5. Missouri—History—
Anecdotes. 6. Missouri—Biography—Anecdotes. 7. Legends—Missouri. 8.
Folklore—Missouri. I. Title.
  GB605.M8W43 2008
  551.44'709778—dc22

                                                                2007037350

Designer: Stephanie Foley
Typesetter: Foley Design
Printer and binder: Thomson-Shore, Inc.
Typefaces: Blackbeard and ITC New Baskerville

To the organized cavers of Missouri, without whose fifty years of dedicated efforts to locate and survey the caves of Missouri we would not have a legacy of more than 6,200 recorded caves;

and

To the show cave developers of Missouri, who have made it possible for everyone to journey underground and enjoy the wonders and curiosities of the Cave State.

CONTENTS

PREFACE

From Ash to Buzzard to Counterfeit, Missouri's varied non-commercial and commercial caves are as endless as the times; as changing as the scenery; as ageless as the Elephant Rocks. Some you have heard about and probably visited. The names and locations of others would come as a surprise to most. And some say there are as many as 350 recorded caves in the Show-Me State!

—*Missouri News Magazine*
(Missouri Division of Resources and Development), 1957

Today, anyone with a computer and an Internet hookup can go online and within a few minutes learn more about half a dozen Missouri caves than was known about all the caves in the state fifty-five years ago. I know because when I was growing up I was hungry for such information and it simply didn't exist. Neither did the home computer or the Internet.

My introduction to Missouri caves came in 1945 at the age of seven when my parents took me to see Mark Twain Cave at Hannibal. We lived at Hannibal for several years before moving to central Missouri. During those years my father got permission to take me on a spelunking (caving) trip into the undeveloped portions of Mark Twain Cave. We also got to explore Cameron Cave, which honeycombs the hill on the opposite side of the valley in which Mark Twain Cave is located.

To say that I became hooked on caves as a result of those adventures would be an understatement. Those cave trips were important

The author, H. Dwight
Weaver (left), at age
sixteen, and his high
school caving buddy,
Robert (Bob) Rothwell,
after exploring Vernon
Cave in Miller County,
1954. *(Photo by Hal
Weaver; from the author's
collection)*

because they filled me with a passion for cave exploration and study
that became a large part of my life for the next fifty-five years.

But it wasn't until I was old enough to get a driver's license that I
could really begin to try to quench my thirst for caves. My father took
me caving only occasionally, but once I had a driver's license and a
car, I was off into the hills of central Missouri almost every weekend
with my buddies, looking for caves. Caves seemed to be just about
everywhere. My favorite areas were the sinkhole regions in Boone
County, which are now Rock Bridge Memorial State Park and the
Three Creeks Conservation Area. I developed my spelunking skills
in two of central Missouri's largest and most spectacular wild caves—
the Devil's Icebox and Hunter's Cave.

From 1945 to 1955, I discovered that caves and the creatures that use them did not receive much respect from most adults in that day and age. They said caves were dark, wet, cold, muddy, worthless holes in the ground. Caves were full of bats, which many people feared and thought were better off dead than alive. Adults said caves were where you would find poisonous snakes lying in wait for you, where a person could get lost, and where the cave ceiling might collapse and bury you alive. Never mind that these impressions were, for the most part, untrue. Such beliefs were very common, and I certainly could not disprove them, because there seemed to be no reliable and easily obtained information on Missouri caves.

Many landowners who had caves on their property considered them a nuisance and liability instead of a valuable resource if they were not pretty enough to be show caves. Most of the owners had not even thoroughly explored their own caves and either did not know or had forgotten how important caves were to their predecessors. Rumor held that every pit cave was bottomless and every wild cave connected with some other cave five or ten miles away. Meanwhile, the guides in show caves were more interested in entertaining visitors than providing useful information. Tour guides in show caves were long on legend and folklore and short on fact and reality.

There were no caving clubs that I could join. There were no books on caves in any of the libraries that I frequented, and no books on caves available in local bookstores. I had endless questions and no answers. So at the age of sixteen, I vowed that since there were no books in the libraries on Missouri caves, I would write them myself. To begin my quest, I sat down and wrote a letter to every state that had a geological survey, requesting any information they might have on caves. I told them that I was doing cave research and was going to write a book.

In the following weeks I got letters and information from nearly two dozen state geological surveys and in the process made contact with the National Speleological Society (NSS). It was a relatively new organization dedicated to the exploration and study of caves. I had never heard of the NSS. I wasn't quite old enough to join, but by 1956 I had become a member, and the NSS put me in touch with other members in Missouri. There weren't very many, but they were in the process of establishing a statewide cave survey. I was fortunate to be in the right place at the right time to become a member of the newly formed Missouri Speleological Survey (MSS).

Thanks to the MSS and its dedicated member groups throughout the state who have spent the past five decades locating, naming, recording, mapping, photographing, and inventorying cave resources, Missouri now has one of the largest sets of cave files of any state in the nation. The archive is filled with reports on more than 6,200 caves, maps on nearly 3,000 of these caves, many photographs, and a great deal of miscellaneous information about Missouri caves statewide. These archives are housed with the records of the Missouri Department of Natural Resources Division of Geology and Land Survey at Rolla, Missouri.

I kept my promise to write those books. This one, *Missouri Caves in History and Legend,* is my sixth book on Missouri caves. Still, misinformation about Missouri caves is plentiful. What I have tried to do in this book is shed some light on the historical significance of Missouri caves and to explore the ways in which people in the past have both used and abused these resources. The expression "out of sight, out of mind" applies well to caves. Except for their entrances, their mysteries, wonders, and curiosities are cloaked in the eternal night of total darkness, and only a small number of people ever give them much serious thought. Half a century ago caves needed friends, because almost nobody understood them or really appreciated them. We've made a lot of progress since the 1950s. But even today, in what we like to think of as our enlightened society, our caves, the resources they contain, and the creatures that live in them still need friends.

ACKNOWLEDGMENTS

Missouri caves have been at the core of my life for nearly sixty years, and many of those years have been spent exploring and doing cave research of one kind or another. None of the stories and books that I have written about Missouri caves sprang fully formed from my imagination. Behind each were individuals and institutions that provided valuable information and support. This book is no exception.

First and foremost I need to thank the countless numbers of cavers, landowners, scientists, state employees, and others whose contributions to the files of the Missouri Speleological Survey over the past fifty years have created an irreplaceable reservoir of information. I am indebted to Scott House for his assistance as well as to that of Matt Forir.

In the effort to produce this book, I wish to thank Laura Jolley of the Missouri State Archives; the Missouri State Library; the State Historical Society of Missouri; William "Bill" Elliott of the Missouri Department of Conservation; Jody Eberly of the U.S. Forest Service; James Vandike of the Missouri Department of Natural Resources Division of Geology and Land Survey; Gordon Smith of the National Cave Museum; Estle Funkhouser and Lloyd and Edith Richardson of Crystal Cave; and all the members of the Missouri Caves Association, who have always been generous in providing assistance.

I also want to thank the individuals who reviewed the manuscript. Their eye to detail and accuracy kept me from making many blunders. There is no substitute for Becky Schroeder. Her knowledge and long years of dedication to the Missouri Heritage Readers series makes working with her both a pleasure and an unforgettable experience. She's the kind of editor every writer needs to have.

There is one more individual that I must acknowledge—my wife, Rosie. As Becky Schroeder said after reading the first draft of this manuscript, "Your love for caves certainly shows in your writing." I may love caves, but Rosie has endured my obsession with caves for nearly fifty years. That is the hallmark of an even greater love.

MISSOURI
CAVES
IN HISTORY
AND LEGEND

Ice Age Bones

A surprisingly large number of Missourians are engaged in cave exploration. . . . These explorers have recently developed a special interest in the bones that are found in many caves, and new finds are reported so rapidly that it is difficult to keep pace with their identification and analysis.

—M. G. MEHL, *Missouri's Ice Age Animals*, 1962

Since the days of the Lewis and Clark Expedition, the bones of ice age animals have been found all across Missouri. They remind us that many great beasts, now extinct, once roamed this land, including creatures such as woolly mammoths, mastodons, giant ground sloths, peccaries (ancient piglike animals), moose-elk, bison, long-legged dire wolves (which must have been terrifying), enormous cave bears, ferocious saber-toothed cats, huge American lions, and giant beavers. A surprisingly large number of fossil animal remains have been found in Missouri caves embedded in clay and gravel sediments. Some remains have been discovered lying exposed on cave floors right where the animal died thousands of years ago. In addition, the clay floors and stream banks of some caves preserve the tracks, dens, and claw marks of extinct animals.

Several decades ago cavers discovered the footprints of the extinct American lion in a cave near the Missouri-Arkansas border. The species has been dead for more than eight thousand years, yet the tracks looked so fresh, according to the cavers, that seeing them raised the hair on the backs of their necks. It was easy to imagine the animal was still alive and somewhere close by in the cave. Many caves

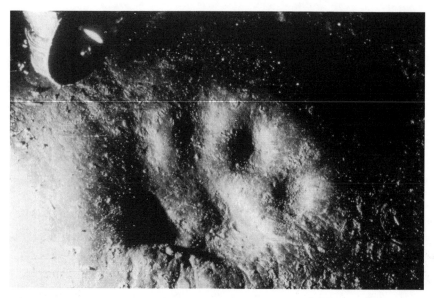

This paw print of the extinct American lion *(Panthera leo atrox)* in cave clay is estimated to be eight thousand years old. The print measures seven and a half inches across. (Courtesy James Vandike)

have the ability to preserve fossil remains and tracks for a very long period of time. Another set of remarkable animal tracks preserved in clay were found in a cave near Perryville south of St. Louis—footprints believed to be those of the ice age jaguar or saber-toothed cat.

These kinds of discoveries make experienced cavers very cautious when exploring a wild cave they have not visited before or a cave known to be virgin. They pay attention to where they put their feet, because fossil imprints left in soft clay can be easily and quickly destroyed. One can only wonder how many fossil tracks of ice age, or Pleistocene Epoch, animals have been destroyed in Missouri caves over the past 150 years by careless people.

A diverse group of large animals existed here between ten thousand and two million years ago. The undisputed champions for size were members of the elephant family. The most abundant were the American mastodons and the more common ice age mammoth. These enormous creatures shared their environment with the giant

North American beaver, a muskratlike animal as large as the modern-day black bear. There were two species of ground sloth, one of them a giant, with enormous claws designed for digging and self-defense. The animal weighed a ton and stood twelve feet high on its hind feet.

Another impressive creature was the giant short-faced cave bear, which stood five and a half feet tall at the shoulders and weighed around fourteen hundred pounds. The bear was a formidable carnivore, but it was not alone as it stalked the herbivorous browsers of savanna, swamp, and woodland. The bear's competition included saber-toothed cats, jaguars, lions, and packs of dire wolves.

These predators fed upon wildlife much different than that of present-day Missouri animals. During the ice age there were also tapirs, armadillos, camels, and crocodiles living in the area that is now Missouri. These animals probably numbered in the millions, and most of them vanished, including the predators, in a relatively short span of time. The issue of why they disappeared so quickly toward the end of the ice age is a subject of considerable scientific debate.

Throughout geologic history there have been many ice ages. The most recent one began about two million years ago. Its cause, like the extinctions of plants and animals, is still highly debatable. Why some animals grew so large during the ice age is also uncertain, but it may have had to do with the nutritional value of the vegetation they consumed and the abundance of good things to eat. Their large size may have also been an adaptation to challenges in the overall environment.

The extinction of these animals may have been caused by the changing climate, but mass extinctions are nothing new. They have occurred a number of times over the past six hundred million years. But while the older extinctions were probably due entirely to natural events unrelated to humans, it appears that some of the extinctions in Missouri did not occur until after the arrival of Native American (Paleo-Indian) groups around ten thousand to fourteen thousand years ago.

Missourians began asking questions about these fossils in the nineteenth century, when the remains kept turning up in newly plowed fields, creek gravel, river sediments, clay banks, and at construction

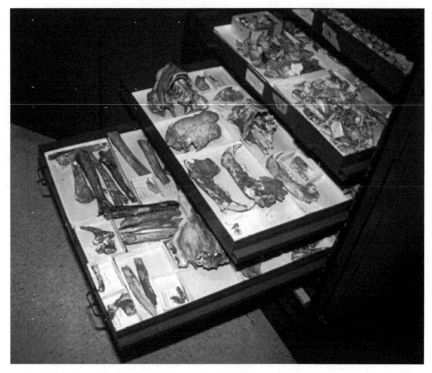

Bones in the Missouri section of the Pleistocene bone collection repository at the Research and Collections Center, Illinois State Museum, Springfield. The specimens in the drawers shown here are some of the first ice age animal bones found by Missouri cavers. (Photo by H. Dwight Weaver, 1996)

sites. Some of the first bones of mastodon, peccary, and ground sloth were excavated in the 1830s in eastern Missouri around Kimmswick.

Today, however, most ice age animal remains are found in caves. Animals such as mammoths and mastodons certainly did not live in caves, but their bones were often washed into caves by storm waters or their carcasses dragged into caves by predators. Sinkhole pits that dropped into caves also served as animal traps. The animals would fall in, be unable to climb out, and die of injuries or starvation. Dire wolves, bears, cats, and a few other animals probably denned in caves and dragged their prey into caves, thus leaving behind a stash of bones for today's cavers to find and paleontologists to study.

One of the most surprising such cave discoveries occurred September 11, 2001, at Springfield, Missouri. On the very day that terrorists were destroying the World Trade Center towers in New York City, a road construction crew discovered a remarkable cave beneath the city streets of Springfield, the largest city in the Missouri Ozarks. Known today as River Bluff Cave, this unique resource contains more than a half mile of passage and is highly decorated with cave formations. It also contains a vast accumulation of ice age animal remains and footprints. Scientists now consider the cave a world-class fossil site, and it may be the oldest fossil cave in North America. This time capsule of the ice age had been sealed by natural events for thousands of years, protecting its fossil remains, which some scientists estimate to be six hundred thousand to one million years old.

The giant short-faced cave bear denned in River Bluff Cave, leaving behind its beds and mighty claw marks as well as a tale of slaughter when it preyed on flat-headed peccaries. The peccaries left behind a rare trail of footprints, bones, and feces in the cave. Even the waste matter of these ancient animals is important because it can tell us what they ate, facts about their environment, and the general nature of their health.

Fossil remains from the cave include mammoth, horse, musk ox, turtles, snakes, and the saber-toothed cat. Since this ice age "museum" has only recently been discovered, its resources have barely been researched. Who knows what discoveries are yet to be made in River Bluff Cave?

Giant cave bears and ice age cats were the first mammals to use caves in the Missouri Ozarks as dens, but mankind too would find refuge in the caves beginning around eleven thousand years ago. Prehistoric cultures would leave behind ceremonial sites, footprints, artwork, fabrics, stone and bone tools and weapons, the remains of countless meals, and even evidence of human burials in Missouri caves.

2

Prehistoric Times

If "Cave Man". . . ever existed in the Mississippi Valley, he would not find any part of its natural features better adapted for his requirements than in the Ozark hills.
—GERARD FOWKE, *Cave Explorations in the Ozark Regions of Central Missouri,* 1922

Because Missouri is at the confluence of the nation's three great heartland rivers, the Mississippi, Missouri, and Ohio, it became a crossroads for America's prehistoric Indian cultures. Scientists estimate that the total number of archaeological sites in Missouri could be in the millions. For some counties alone, there are more than two thousand recorded sites, according to Missouri archaeologist Larry Grantham.

Water, to a large extent, determined where prehistoric groups settled or had temporary campsites. It had a major impact upon their environment, their food, and their physical prosperity. These factors, in turn, influenced their social structure, material culture, religion, and trade patterns. Prehistoric Indians, like the American and European settlers who came after them, tended to live along rivers and close to freshwater spring outlets. Missouri caves and rock shelters are most frequently found in bluffs, in sinkhole basins, and along hillsides of streams and rivers. Spring outlets, regardless of their size, are simply cave openings that discharge groundwater.

By definition, a cave generally has an opening that is deeper than it is wide and penetrates the hill, whereas a rock shelter is a hollow that is generally wider than it is deep without a cave component.

Entrance to Graham Cave in Graham Cave State Park in Montgomery County. Artifacts found at this site indicate the cave was used by Paleo-Indians as a shelter and ceremonial site eleven thousand years ago. In 1961 this cave became the first archaeological site in the United States to be designated a National Historic Landmark. (Photo by H. Dwight Weaver, 1990)

There are exceptions since both characteristics can be part of the same natural feature or closely associated with it. There are many rock shelter archaeological sites throughout Missouri and many of them have produced prehistoric materials. The number of cave sites that contain prehistoric material is definitely fewer in number. Yet some cave sites are highly significant because cave environments often preserve materials for a long period of time. This depends, of course, upon the composition of the prehistoric material. Good examples are the finds at Arnold Research Cave, also known as Saltpeter Cave, in Callaway County.

John Phillips, one of the first settlers of Callaway County, settled near the present town of Portland and took possession of this cave in 1816 for the purpose of making gunpowder from the cave's saltpeter deposits. The cave subsequently became known as Saltpeter

Cave. Some years later, H. E. Arnold came into possession of the Saltpeter Cave property, and by the early twentieth century the cave was known as Arnold Cave. Long noted for the beauty of its entrance, which has a graceful arch of sandstone spanning two hundred feet, the entry chamber leads to several additional rooms within the hill that are connected by low-ceiling crawlways.

Professional archaeological excavation began at the cave in the mid-1950s. Since then it has been called Arnold Research Cave. The excavations resulted in the discovery of prehistoric materials dating back seven thousand to ten thousand years. Among the finds were more than thirty specimens of perfectly preserved moccasins and slip-on shoes estimated to be nine thousand years old. The moccasins were made of leather while the other shoe-types were woven from fibrous plants. Such finds are uncommon, because most archaeological sites yield only prehistoric materials made of stone and bone. The dry, dusty condition of the cave deposits containing the preservative elements of saltpeter may have been partially responsible for the excellent state of preservation of the shoes.

Not far away, in adjacent Montgomery County, is Graham Cave, which was formed in the same St. Peter Sandstone formation as Arnold Research Cave. Graham Cave, however, does not have internal chambers and is more easily classified as a rock shelter. It is now the centerpiece of Graham Cave State Park. Artifacts found in the shelter cave are as much as ten thousand years old, according to radiocarbon dating technology.

Archaeologists have divided the span of time between the appearance of the first Indians in Missouri and the arrival of European settlers into periods that reflect major cultural advances among these vanished people. They include the hunters of the Paleo-Indian Period, 12,000–8000 BC; the hunter-foragers of the Dalton Period, 8000–7000 BC; the foragers of the Archaic Period, 7000–1000 BC; the prairie-forest potters of the Woodland periods, 1000 BC–AD 900; and the village farmers of the Mississippian periods, AD 900–1700.

Most of these cultures used caves from time to time as campsites, as refuges from winter cold and summer heat, as a source for flint to make weapons and tools, and as a source of water, clay for pottery, and minerals that had ceremonial and medicinal uses. Native

Americans left pictographs (prehistoric drawings or paintings) and petroglyphs (prehistoric carvings and inscriptions) on some Missouri cave walls. According to Carol Diaz-Granados and James R. Duncan, in *The Petroglyphs and Pictographs of Missouri,* about one-third of Missouri's known rock-art sites are "located on the inner or outer walls of caves and rock shelters."

Very few people think of Missouri caves as graveyards, but some caves contain Indian burials. Such burials are of special interest to professional archaeologists and their associates in their pursuit of the secrets of Missouri's prehistoric past. Unfortunately, the burials are also of interest to unethical collectors who seek Indian artifacts and grave goods for profit. Professional archaeologists have a word they use to describe unprincipled, profit-motivated artifact collectors—*looters.* These grave robbers seldom keep records of their finds and make no effort to report their discoveries.

No one knows for certain just how many of Missouri's current 6,200 recorded caves contain Indian burials. In order to protect the cave resources from looters, no list of such caves has been made public. But it is safe to assume that scores of Missouri caves have yielded Indian remains over the past two hundred years.

Early European and American settlers who mined Missouri caves for saltpeter were probably the first to happen upon prehistoric burial sites, because they had reason to excavate cave soils. From the beginning of European settlement, it was "open season" on Indian artifacts and graves. The collecting of antiquities, as Indian artifacts were then commonly called, evolved into a popular pastime. Digging in caves to find artifacts and burials became a popular activity, and the market for antiquities blossomed. The average antiquities collector in the late 1800s and early 1900s felt no regret about plundering artifact sites and taking Native American grave goods and body parts because of their belief that the Indians were uncivilized and racially inferior to whites.

Unfortunately, elements of this attitude have survived to the present day, because Indian artifact and burial sites in Missouri caves are still the focus of looters, who often do their digging at night or with posted lookouts during the daytime. They operate in the Ozark hills in much the same fashion as moonshiners once did and metham-

Gerard Fowke, the first archaeologist to seriously investigate Missouri caves for Indian burials. In 1818 and 1819, he explored scores of caves, former Indian village sites, and burial mounds along the major streams of south-central Missouri. (Ohio State Archaeological and Historical Society; courtesy State Historical Society of Missouri, Columbia)

phetamine manufacturers do today, creating a dangerous situation for anyone who might happen upon them unexpectedly.

Digging up Indian artifact and burial sites on federal or Indian tribal land without proper authority is in violation of federal law, in particular the Native American Graves Protection and Repatriation of Cultural Patrimony Act (November 1990). Even digging up unmarked graves on private land or in caves in Missouri without the proper authority is a violation of Missouri law. Missouri law defines such burials as "any instance where human skeletal remains are discovered or are believed to exist, but for which there exists no written historical documentation or grave markers." If you knowingly disturb, destroy, or damage an unmarked human burial site, you are committing a class D felony, which can result in imprisonment and a fine.

Archaeologist Gerard Fowke, a tall, stern, independent man of frugal habits and eccentric behavior, was the first scientist to seriously investigate Missouri caves for Indian burials. In 1918 and 1919, he explored scores of caves, former Indian village sites, and burial mounds along the major streams of south-central Missouri. He was searching for evidence to support a theory that the ancestors of Native American cultures migrated to the United States from Asia.

The caves Fowke examined were largely along the banks of the Gasconade and Osage rivers and their tributaries. His report was published in 1922 in Bulletin 76 of the Smithsonian Institution, Bureau of American Ethnology. It is interesting to read because of his social commentary, recording folklore as well as fact. He found many human bones and skulls in the caves he excavated, although antiquities collectors and curious local people had excavated in some of the caves long before Fowke's arrival. When he examined Ramsey's Cave along the Big Piney River, he recorded a story about a naive local man who had a joke played on him while digging for artifacts in a cave. The story illustrates the attitudes of many of our ancestors toward Indian remains versus the remains of white people.

"A man living near the cave reported that a few years ago he was digging in a narrow space between the east wall and a large fallen rock," said Fowke. "He came upon the feet of two skeletons and took out the lower leg bones. Being assured by a friend that these were not bones of Indians because they were not 'red,' and so must be the remains of white people, he replaced them and threw the earth back on them."

Both archaeologists and looters are concerned primarily with Indians who placed their dead in caves. But in the 1800s, after the arrival of Americans and Europeans, bodies of several white people also wound up in caves through some spooky and bizarre happenings.

3

Spooky Burials

There is a wide difference in human interest about caves.
—WALTER B. STEVENS,
Missouri: The Center State, 1821–1915

The early settlers of the Ozarks sometimes took shelter in dry caves, which they would occupy until such time as it was possible to build a cabin. In most instances, these settlers were not later buried in the caves, but one named John Wilson was. John Wilson came to the Ozarks in 1810 from Hopkins County, Kentucky. He found a cave in a bluff along the Barren Fork of the Big Tavern Creek, in territory that would eventually become Miller County. He proceeded to set up housekeeping in the big, dry cave with his wife, Nellie (Ray), and their three sons, Alexander, William, and Willis.

Affectionately called "Jack" by most of the people who knew him, John was considered eccentric even in his day. He got along well with the Osage Indians, with whom he traded, and he even learned to speak their language. He and his family resided in the cave for two years before John got around to putting up a cabin. He made his living by hunting, raising hogs, and farming the Tavern Creek bottoms, where he raised Indian corn, beans, and pumpkins.

As John aged, he became increasingly eccentric and more attached to the old cave that had sheltered him and his family for two years. The Wilson cabin stood very near the cave. His wife, however, did not share his sentiments about the cave. When John began to talk about being buried in the cave, his wife objected. She preferred a more conventional burial site. John's wife preceded him in death and so did their sons Alexander and William. These two sons had married and remained close to home, but the other son, Willis, moved from Miller County after marriage.

John did not bury his wife and two deceased sons in the cave, but alone now and well along in years, he began to dwell upon his own demise and began making preparations for his death and funeral. He built his own coffin. He recorded elaborate plans for how his body was to be prepared after death. His vital organs and entrails were to be removed, and his body cavities packed with salt. He thought this procedure would preserve his body and cause it to pet-rify. He instructed his two closest friends, Silas Capps and Daniel Cummings, to place his body in the coffin, packed with salt. He wanted his coffin then to be sealed up in a cavity just to the right of the big cave entrance at about cave ceiling height. Two demijohns (large, narrow-necked bottles) of peach brandy were also to be sealed in with him. He wanted his funeral procession to be led by fiddlers playing the "Eighth of January." After seven years his tomb was to be unsealed, his petrified body propped up inside the cave, and his friends were to drink the peach brandy and have a great party with him present to enjoy the festivities.

John Wilson died August 22, 1856, and his body was prepared for burial just as he wished. Dr. John A. P. Nixdorf Sr. of Eldon and Dr. John Brockman of Tuscumbia prepared his body. The burial proce-dure that followed was the most unusual interment ever witnessed in Miller County's early days. Unfortunately, John Wilson did not fore-see the Civil War, which began before the seven years expired and brought such disruption that Miller County people forgot all about John Wilson. Legend relates, however, that sometime after the war, some of his old friends remembered him. They visited the cave and discovered that grave robbers had been at work. The tomb was unsealed and the peach brandy was gone, but John's coffin and body were still there. He was then buried next to his wife and chil-dren elsewhere in Miller County.

John Wilson's belief that his body would petrify after death, if pre-pared as he instructed, was a fairly common belief held in the 1800s. Petrification—preserving the body by making it rigid or inert like stone—was a topic of much interest to intellectuals. John Wilson

Dr. Joseph Nash McDowell established one of the first medical colleges west of the Mississippi River. In the 1840s, he performed gruesome medical experiments on the body of one of his deceased children in Mark Twain Cave at Hannibal. (State Historical Society of Missouri, Columbia)

may have been living in the backwoods of Miller County, but he was obviously not out of touch with the issues of his day.

Another eccentric individual of Wilson's time also chose a Missouri cave for an experiment, resulting in one of the most bizarre incidents ever to involve a Missouri cave and a human burial. The man who performed the experiment was Dr. Joseph Nash McDowell, who established one of the first medical colleges west of the Mississippi in 1838 in St. Louis. His school was the original medical department of Kemper College, which was in operation until 1845. After the college closed, McDowell reorganized his school as the Missouri Medical College.

McDowell, born in Lexington, Kentucky, April 1, 1805, followed the family tradition and became a medical doctor. His formal education was at Transylvania College in Kentucky, where he studied under Dr. Samuel Brown, the school's professor of chemistry and medical subjects. Brown was an authority on saltpeter and the saltpeter caves of Kentucky, and he not only conducted experiments with saltpeter but also encouraged his students to do so. Brown thought the preservative qualities of saltpeter had promising medical uses.

In McDowell's time, obtaining a cadaver (a dead body intended for dissection for medical research) was nearly impossible. So he did business with "resurrectionists"—men who were considered ghouls because they would steal newly buried bodies from graveyards to sell on the black market for medical experimentation. It was this activity, coupled with McDowell's belief in spiritualism and ghosts, that revealed the darker side of his character.

In 1827, McDowell married Amanda Virginia Drake of Mason County, Kentucky. She bore him ten children. More than one child did not survive childhood diseases, and because bodies were so difficult to obtain, McDowell dissected and performed experiments on his own dead children. Seeking a place where he could establish an underground laboratory for experiments, he heard about a cave just south of Hannibal, Missouri, called Saltpeter Cave. He visited the site and was so impressed that he bought the cave. This was in the late 1840s at the time when Samuel Clemens was growing up in Hannibal. Sam and his buddies were familiar with Saltpeter Cave in Cave Hollow. It was where the local youths often spent their free time playing in the cave's confusing maze of tunnels. But McDowell did not know this.

In later years, after Samuel Clemens became the celebrated author Mark Twain and used the cave for a setting in some of his books, he commented upon McDowell's purchase of the cave. In *Life on the Mississippi,* Twain said: "In my time the person who owned it [the cave] turned it into a mausoleum for his daughter, age fourteen. The body of this poor child was put in a copper cylinder filled with alcohol, and this suspended in one of the dismal avenues of the cave." McDowell had placed a stout door over the main entrance to the cave to keep people out but was unaware that it had other, lesser-known, entrances. Twain told of how local "rowdies" would sneak into the cave and drag the girl's body up by her hair to look at her.

In *Missouri: The Center State,* Walter B. Stevens also gave an account of McDowell's strange experiment:

> He had very strange ideas about the disposition of the dead. . . .
> A child of Dr. McDowell died. . . . The coffin was lined with
> metal. The body was placed in the coffin. All space remaining
> was filled with alcohol and the coffin was tightly sealed. A year
> or so later the body of the child was removed from the coffin
> and placed in a large copper case. This was McDowell's method
> of treating the bodies of his children. No religious service of any
> kind was performed. The copper cases were carried at night
> attended by a procession formed by the medical students and
> friends of the family. Each person carried a torch. The place of
> disposition was a vault in the rear of the residence. The thought
> of a natural cave as a final resting place was a favorite one. Dr.
> McDowell bought the cave near Hannibal. . . . The vase or case
> containing one of the children was taken from St. Louis to this
> cave and suspended from the roof.

The girl's body hung in the cave for two years, but the youths who sneaked into the cave to view her bragged about it to their friends, and ugly rumors spread through Hannibal about the weird activities of McDowell in Cave Hollow. Alarmed, local men stormed the place, broke down the door, and took a look for themselves. McDowell was then forced to remove the body of the girl from the cave and to cease using the cave for such experiments.

Saltpeter Cave became known as McDowell's Cave during McDowell's ownership. After Mark Twain's books about the adventures of Tom Sawyer and Huckleberry Finn became popular, people began calling it Mark Twain Cave. The popularity of Twain's books also brought public demands for access to the cave, and it was commercialized in 1886. It is the oldest show cave operation west of the Mississippi River. The remote area within Mark Twain Cave where McDowell's strange experiment took place more than 120 years ago is not regularly shown to the touring public today, but it was briefly part of the cave's evening candlelight tours in the mid-1970s. The eerie underground location and the telling of the story was always a spooky highlight of the tours for children and adults alike.

Missouri caves abound in seldom-told tales and unsolved mysteries. Many subjects related to their history have seen very little research, partially because documentation is difficult to come by. A good example is the saltpeter and gunpowder enterprises that occurred in and were associated with Missouri caves between 1720 and 1820.

4

Saltpeter and Gunpowder

In the spring of 1810, James McDonald, of Bonhomme, and his
two sons went to some caves on the Gasconade River to make
saltpeter, and in three weeks returned to St. Louis with 3,000
pounds.

—WILLIAM CLARK BRECKENRIDGE,
Missouri Historical Review, October 1925

Historians have long thought that Hernando de Soto, who died
in Arkansas in 1542 during his famous sixteenth-century expedition into North America, did not reach present-day Missouri. But
in 1993, a commission of prominent de Soto scholars released newly
translated, controversial, four-hundred-year-old Spanish accounts
that said otherwise.

According to Donald E. Sheppard, one of the scholars who traced
de Soto's Missouri route, the de Soto expedition found salt (sodium
chloride) at Saline Creek, near St. Mary's in the southeast corner of
Ste. Genevieve County. They first found saltpeter (potassium
nitrate) near Pilot Knob (west of Ironton), and then again near the
White River in the Branson neighborhood while they were traveling
toward Arkansas. The area they passed through between Forsyth
and today's Arkansas border is a cavernous region. In what cave they
found saltpeter is presently uncertain, but it may have been Bear
Den Cave not far from Reed's Spring. A saltpeter mining operation
functioned at this cave as early as 1835, supplying material for one
of the first powder mills in southwest Missouri.

The conquistadors' discovery of saltpeter in Missouri is of historic

Entrance to Rocheport Cave near the Missouri River in Boone County. First mentioned by members of the Lewis and Clark Expedition, this cave was the site of a saltpeter and gunpowder manufacturing plant in 1811. In the 1960s, it was a show cave, operated as Boone Cave. Today it is a gated sanctuary for endangered bats under the management of the Missouri Department of Conservation. (Photo by Ralph Walker; courtesy Missouri State Archives)

importance. The Missouri sites were the only places, according to Sheppard, where Hernando de Soto's people found saltpeter in North America. In the years that followed, saltpeter miners became the first Europeans to place a memorable stamp upon the history of Missouri caves. In Missouri, the two backwoods operations—saltpeter mining and gunpowder making—generally went hand in hand and often took place on the same property. It was a dangerous process, and in pioneer times many powder mills exploded and people were killed because their methods and tools were crude.

Missouri public records show that "Jack Maupin had a powder plant on the Meramec River in a cave and supplied trappers with most of their munitions. Fisher's Cave, Saltpeter Cave [Meramec Caverns], and Copper Hollow Cave, all . . . near Sullivan, were famous powder making plants from 1810 to 1820." Apparently another member of the Maupin family had a powder plant near Dundee in Franklin County, but according to an early historian, his plant exploded.

Saltpeter, also known as *niter,* is potassium (or sodium) nitrate. When it is combined and ground together with charcoal and sulfur, correctly and in just the right quantities, it produces black gunpowder. The making of gunpowder in Missouri in pioneer times relied largely on the mining of saltpeter earth ("peter dirt") from caves, and the process for making it was common knowledge at that time.

Not all cave soils contain saltpeter, and how the soils of some caves become charged with this substance has long been a mystery. Even today scientists are not entirely certain about the origin of saltpeter in caves. Various theories explain its origin; one explanation is that groundwater seepage brings nitrates into the cave from surface soils. Another theory suggests that species of bacteria and other microorganisms enrich the cave with nitrates. Still another explanation points to the waste matter of bats and rodents, which is high in nitrates; since certain species of both animals use Missouri caves as a habitat, their waste deposits can enrich the cave soil.

Saltpeter miners often placed the peter dirt in triangular wooden vats or hoppers, then poured water on top of the dirt. As the water seeped down through the dirt, it collected (leached) nitrates. The nitrate-rich water dripped into a trough at the bottom of the hopper,

The entrance of Arnold Research Cave, near Portland in Callaway County. John Phillips, one of the first settlers of Callaway County, operated a saltpeter mining operation and gunpowder plant at this cave from 1816 to 1825. Archaeologists excavated the artifact-rich sediments of the cave in the 1960s. About twenty years ago, a former owner bulldozed much natural fill from the cave. The opening is now twenty feet high at the center and two hundred feet wide. (Photo by H. Dwight Weaver, 1998)

which drained into a large kettle. This liquid was then heated, and the water boiled away, leaving small, white, needlelike crystals of saltpeter in the bottom of the kettles. The crystals were then used to make gunpowder. Saltpeter crystals have a cool, bitter taste and will flash if tossed into a fire.

Missouri has nineteen caves called "Saltpeter Cave" and several more with the word *saltpeter* in the cave's name. Counties that have one cave each by the name Saltpeter include Callaway, Crawford, Dallas, Douglas, Franklin, Laclede, Madison, McDonald, Phelps, Shannon, Ste. Genevieve, Stone, and Texas. Dent County has two caves called Saltpeter, and Pulaski County has four. Having the word *saltpeter* in its name does not mean that a cave was mined for saltpeter, yet it probably does mean that at some early date saltpeter deposits were recognized in the cave.

"Saltpeter" is a nineteenth-century name for a cave. Because early Missouri settlers needed saltpeter and searched caves for it between 1720 and 1820, caves in which it was found often became locally known by the name. Some caves in Missouri that were once called "Saltpeter Cave" have since been given another name. These caves include Ashley's Cave in Dent County; Boiling Spring Cave in Pulaski County; Indian Cave in Franklin County; Arnold Research Cave in Callaway County; Temple of Wisdom Cave in Crawford County; Fisher Cave, Copper Hollow Cave, and Meramec Caverns in Franklin County; Friede's Cave in Phelps County; Bear Den Cave in Stone County; Rocheport Cave in Boone County; Mark Twain Cave in Marion County; Marsh Creek Cave No. 1 in Madison County; and Firey Forks Cave in Camden County.

Unfortunately, records of saltpeter mining are very scarce because most backwoods operators never made an official report of their activities. There are probably many additional caves in Missouri that were mined for saltpeter but have escaped the notice of historians. One might suppose that the War of 1812 and the Civil War stimulated considerable saltpeter mining and gunpowder making in Missouri caves, but there is very little evidence to indicate that such was the case. Carol A. Hill, an authority on saltpeter mining in North American caves, states that Missouri was not an important producer of gunpowder during either war.

Saltpeter mining in caves in the Appalachian Mountains began at Clark's Saltpeter Cave in Virginia about 1740. It probably began in Missouri shortly after 1720, initiated by Philip Renault, who established himself at Kaskaskia, Illinois, in that year and began mining lead in Missouri west of Ste. Genevieve. "It is probable that from the year 1720 when Renault and La Motte opened and worked the lead mines in this region on a large scale and roasted the ores therefrom to eliminate the sulphur that they, as well as those who came after them . . . made their own gunpowder, using the waste product sulphur in its manufacture," wrote William Breckenridge in a 1925 issue of the *Missouri Historical Review.*

Folklore of the area credits Renault with the discovery of

Meramec Caverns, originally known as Saltpeter Cave, today a show cave near Stanton. "Saltpeter Cave is a large opening below Fisher's Cave. It is entered from near the river. . . . Gunpowder was made in this cave at an early date," according to an early Franklin County historian.

The powder mill operation headquartered at Meramec Caverns and operated by Renault existed between 1720 and 1760. The plant, however, may not have been in continuous operation during all four decades. The operation involved a network of caves producing salt-peter along the Meramec River. The labor force probably consisted of black slaves. It was quite possibly the most productive powder mill to operate in Missouri between 1720 and 1820. Since no production figures are available for the Meramec Caverns powder mill, how it ranks against the better-known powder mill established by William H. Ashley in a Dent County cave in 1814 is unknown.

William Henry Ashley, born in Virginia about 1778, was a fur trader, miner, politician, and frontier entrepreneur. He came to Missouri in 1802, applied himself to various enterprises, got into financial trouble, and then became a lieutenant colonel during the War of 1812. On one of his hunting trips in the Ozarks during the war, he happened upon a large cave in Dent County and discovered that it contained ample deposits of saltpeter dirt. He thought that by establishing a powder plant and saltpeter works, he could make enough money to solve his financial problems.

Colonel Ashley went into partnership with General Benjamin Howard, a fellow military man in the territory, and they began min-ing saltpeter at the big cave, which subsequently became known as Ashley's Cave. It was operated in conjunction with Ashley's powder mill at Potosi. At the start, production was about three thousand pounds per year, worth about twenty thousand dollars, but the salt-peter deposits at Ashley's Cave were extremely sensitive and given to unexpected and deadly flash explosions. The factory at the cave was destroyed three times by explosions, and on one occasion a wagon carrying saltpeter exploded and killed several men. By 1818, the market for gunpowder had fallen on hard times and the cave pow-der mill operation was abandoned. After giving up his powder mills, Ashley had much better financial success when he established the

Rocky Mountain Fur Company, which was associated with such early American explorers as Jedediah Smith, William Sublette, and Jim Bridger, members of "Ashley's Hundred," young men who answered his call to go west to make their fortunes.

Well into the twentieth century, Ashley's Cave continued to have problems. In April 1930, the *Crane Chronicle* newspaper reported that "a brand of fire" had probably struck the entrance of Ashley's Cave, causing an explosion and fire. "But it was only another peculiar and unexplained incident in connection with this century old powder plant," the paper reported. The ground at the cave, according to the article, is still heavily charged with saltpeter, charcoal, and sulphur, which might be ignited by a dart of lightning.

A caver, hunter, or hiker who might happen upon an Ozark cave once mined for saltpeter would be wise not to light a match or start a fire in the cave or take shelter in the cave entrance during a storm that produces lightning. This would be especially true at Ashley's Cave, which has three entrances.

Nevertheless, according to folklore, hunters have used Ashley's Cave since settlement days as a campsite and refuge against unexpected storms. In the early 1800s, many hunting parties were in pursuit of bear, and some hunters may have probed Ashley's Cave for wild game. Bear hunting in Ozark caves was a popular pastime in the first half of the nineteenth century.

5

Bear Hunting

From a cavern in Boone County . . . skeleton material represent-
ing a dozen or more individual bears of this species [*Ursus
americanus*] has been collected by Professor Elder of the
University of Missouri.
—M. G. MEHL, *Missouri's Ice Age Animals,* 1962

Before the arrival of American and European settlers, black bears
were common throughout Missouri, particularly in the Ozark
region. The bears were becoming rare in the woodlands by the
1850s and were gone from most of the state by the 1880s, victims of
habitat loss and overhunting. Their demise left behind a strong
body of folklore and a host of place-names. Robert L. Ramsay, in *Our
Storehouse of Missouri Place Names* (1952), says there are more than
five hundred localities within the state that derive their names from
eight of the larger game animals, and prominent among these is
the bear.

Indeed, the Great Seal of Missouri carries the image of bears.
More than 127 places in Missouri have been named for the bears.
These places include branches, creeks, hollows, springs, ridges, cemeteries, schools, quarries, townships, mountains, sloughs, and caves. In
fact, forty-three caves in Missouri have the word *bear* as the first word
in their names. No other geographic feature in the state makes a
greater use of the word. Among these are the names Bear Cave (the
most common), Bear Bed Cave, Bear Cave System, Bear Creek Cave,
Bear Den Cave, Bear Hole Cave, Bear Hollow Cave, Bear Mountain
Cave, Bear Tooth Cave, Bear Track Cave, Bear Waller Cave, and Bear

Claw Cave. Some of the names are associated with more than one cave, and the caves are scattered across twenty-three counties, most of them in the southern half of the state. Shannon County, with eleven "bear" caves, has the most, followed by Ozark County with four, and Taney, Crawford, and Camden counties with three each.

Because bears became extinct in Missouri by 1890, the word *bear* generally indicates that the cave was named before that date. Many of these names probably originated when bears were seen in the vicinity of the caves or were found wintering in them.

Bear hunting was considered great sport in the Ozarks in the early part of the 1800s. When Henry Rowe Schoolcraft made his historic trip through the wilderness of the Ozarks in 1818, he commented on the relationship between bears and the settlers he found along the way, particularly in the White River country. He found one set-tlement occupied by several families of primitive, backwoods hunters, who, he said, could only talk of bears, hunting, and the like.

Schoolcraft described how these hunters would track an animal to its den during the winter by following its tracks in the snow or by using dogs. If they found the bear in a cave, they would shoot him there or send in the dogs "to provoke him to battle; thus he is either brought in sight within the cave, or driven entirely out of it." Schoolcraft noted that a shot through the heart was necessary because "a shot through the flank, thigh, shoulder, or even the neck does not kill him but provokes him to the utmost rage, and some-times four or five shots are necessary to kill him."

Occasionally the bear hunters met with accident, such as the one that, according to folklore, befell Sylvestre Labaddie Sr. in a Franklin County cave that has ever since carried his name. As the story goes, Labaddie and his son Sylvestre Labaddie Jr. followed a wounded bear to the cave. Labaddie Sr. crawled in, thinking that the bear's wound was mortal. The son waited for hours. When his father did not return, he went back to St. Louis and summoned rescuers, but they were unable to relocate the cave. Some years later, accord-ing to legend, the skeletons of the hunter and the bear were found in Labaddie Cave. Some historians take issue with this story because records show that Sylvestre Labaddie Sr. died in St. Louis in 1794 of natural causes.

Head of the Pleistocene giant short-faced bear (from *Missouri's Ice Age Animals*, by M. G. Mehl, Missouri Department of Business and Administration, Division of Geological Survey and Water Resources, 1962)

Nearly forty years after this supposed bear-hunting accident, *The Youth's Literary Gazette* (1833) published a bear story about a Frenchman and his son that may be the origin of the Labaddie legend. According to this account, after the hunter crawled into the cave, he shot the wounded bear again. The bear, in its attempt to escape, tried to crawl out of the cave and became stuck in the small entrance. There the bear died, trapping the hunter inside the cave. Because there were no roads in the area and the hunter's son had not observed the landmarks well, he could not guide rescuers back to the cave. His father subsequently died in the cave, unable to get past the bear's carcass.

Because hunting wintering bears in Ozark caves was such a popular sport in the early days of exploration and settlement, folklore would have us believe that just about every cave in the Ozarks was first discovered by bear hunters and their dogs. The oldest records of bear in Missouri caves are those of the giant, short-faced cave bear (genus *Arctotherium*) that inhabited the Ozarks during the ice age. But most bear specimens unearthed in Missouri caves are those of the common black bear *(Ursus americanus)*. So many remains have been found that it is obvious these bears routinely wintered in the caves and often in groups.

The absence of bears in Missouri woodlands after 1890 made them popular attractions at city zoos in the decades that followed. But a zoo established in Meramec State Park south of St. Louis near Sullivan in the 1930s came very close to reintroducing bears in the woodlands along the Meramec River in Franklin County.

The 6,800-acre park was established in 1928. Caves and springs are among the park's most outstanding features. In 1930, Sheep Cave became a holding pen for bears, foxes, and raccoons. By the summer of 1933, it had been renamed Bear Den Cave and converted exclusively into a bear den. "Four Missouri black bears are kept there now" the local newspaper reported. Mating in captivity, one bear gave birth to cubs in 1936. The park attendants were elated, and the local paper reported the event in detail.

The late Eddie Miller, who for many decades was the general manager of Bridal Cave at the Lake of the Ozarks, grew up in Franklin County. He was born at Sullivan in 1911 and raised on a farm just outside the boundaries of Meramec State Park. In 1936, he worked at the park taking care of boat rentals, the bathing beach, and other concession duties. He became personally acquainted with the bears. In 1937, Eddie assumed responsibility for Fisher Cave, the park's show cave operation. Like any good cave entrepreneur, he was always looking for new ways to entertain his visitors. He soon discovered a way to use the bears on his cave tours. In 1975, Eddie told the author about his experiences with Fisher Cave and the park bears.

According to Eddie, the park had two bear cubs that broke out of the zoo and couldn't be found. That winter they hibernated in some cave in the park and showed up the next spring nearly full-grown. The bears got into a fight and one killed the other. "He was loose for a long time," said Eddie. "He must have been about three years old when I got acquainted with him. He would raid the garbage cans in the park."

One day when the Fisher Cave gate was open, Eddie saw the bear go into the cave, so he locked him in overnight. "I figured he'd make a lot of tracks in the cave and it would be a good attraction," Eddie said. "I don't think the park superintendent ever knew about it. But I had beautiful bear tracks all over the place."

On another occasion when Eddie locked the bear in the cave overnight, he had an early-morning tour the next day of about a dozen people, and they encountered the bear, unexpectedly, underground. The tour group had no idea there was actually a live bear in the cave. Eddie had told them, but they thought he was joking. "I caught a glimpse of that bear going around a corner just ahead of us," Eddie said. Fisher Cave is not electrically lighted. It is shown using hand-held lanterns, which made seeing the bear difficult.

The bear stayed just out of sight until the tour group reached a place where the cave passage narrows and the ceiling lowers. That's when the bear turned around. "Here he came," said Eddie, "right down the passageway, just a-snorting and rearing. He thought he was getting trapped or pinned down, and he was mad. He was a grown bear, and I figured we'd better let him have his way: 'Give him room!' I shouted. 'Give him room!'

"The people were scared to death. There was one woman who just froze, right in the bear's way. She was so scared she wet all over herself. She just couldn't move, so I jumped over and grabbed her by the arm and jerked her out of the bear's way and off the walk. That bear came right on and just shot right past us. That was the last time I ever locked a bear in Fisher Cave overnight."

Now, nearly seventy years later, we have bears once again in Missouri, but not from Meramec State Park's failed attempt to keep bears in a zoo. The bears have migrated north from the Arkansas portion of the Ozarks into southern Missouri. Missouri Department of Conservation officials believe we now have about three hundred bears living in some forty-nine counties. They have presented no problems and are protected by law.

During early settlement, once homesteaders determined that

there were no bears in a cave on their property, they often began using caves for a variety of farm and home needs, such as a spring-house or a barn.

6

Farm and Home

**During early settlement and development of the Ozarks . . .
springs were used as domestic and stock water supplies; many
springs also became the sites of grist mills, which were the hub
of many community activities.**
—JERRY D. VINEYARD AND GERALD L. FEDER,
Springs of Missouri, 1982

C aves often served as springhouses to store food for Ozark
dwellers. Even though rural electrification came to Missouri in
the 1930s and 1940s, there were many areas in the Ozarks where
homes and farms did not receive electrical service until the early
1950s.

Many Ozarkers continued to use spring- and cave-water supply systems even after the arrival of electricity, drilled wells, and sub-
mersible pumps, because the old cave systems could be used to
water livestock. But the springhouse was a necessity in the days
before electricity and artificial refrigeration were available. Meats
were generally dried or salted and smoked. Vegetables and fruits
could be dried, pickled, or canned. But milk, cheese, and butter had
to be kept cool, and the springhouse provided a means of refrigeration that greatly extended the life of such perishable foods because
caves and springs in the Ozarks have a year-round temperature of
56–60 degrees.

There are thousands of springs in the Ozarks. By the time electricity came to the Ozarks, there were also thousands of springhouses
scattered through the hills and hollows. Since many of them were

Entrance of Bockman Spring Cave, in the Mark Twain National Forest in Oregon County. The cave's spring-fed stream was a source of water for homesteaders. In the past, the cave's opening was walled up with native rock, presumably to protect the water supply from contamination and to provide cool storage for milk, butter, and other foods. (Courtesy U.S. Forest Service)

built of stone, brick, or concrete, it is still possible to find these abandoned relics of the past, although they are becoming scarce. Springhouses were either built over the spring outlet or over the spring branch so that the cold water would flow through a rock or concrete trough inside the springhouse. Water entered on one side of the building and exited on the other. Milk and butter in cans or jars would be set in the water that flowed in the trough. Shelves around the sides of the springhouse provided storage for other food items. The water inlet and outlet would be screened to keep animals out of the building.

When a cave was available, it was often used as a springhouse if the cave entrance was not too large and could be walled up to keep animals out. Dams were also built inside many caves (or at the entrance) to impound the flow of a spring-fed cave stream. However, not all cave streams are fed by perennial springs, and some flow only during (or for a short time after) a rainfall. Caves were still being converted into springhouses and domestic water supplies as late as the 1950s. The entrance of Leech Spring Cave in Oregon County has a small dam across it with a pipe and the initials LMC, which stand for Lloyd M. Cooper, and the date 1955 is etched into the concrete. McDowell Cave, in the same county, was once used as a fruit cellar. In 1981 it still had a low stone wall, flagstones, and the remains of a garden and other ruins. Inside the entrance of McDowell Cave, in the concrete among the flagstones, was etched "May 23, 1941, Utah McDowell, Wilderness, Missouri."

More than two hundred caves in the Ozarks still bear evidence that they were once used for such purposes as food storage. Such evidence consists of crumbling dams, walled-up entrances with doorways, pipes, concrete- and rock-walled troughs, dilapidated shelving, platforms, and old water tanks and abandoned hydraulic rams. There are even a few Ozark caves with interior dams and reservoirs that are still providing water for livestock.

Taney County has nineteen caves with surviving ruins that attest to their use for water supply and cool storage. Oregon County has sixteen such caves, Pulaski County fifteen, Christian County fourteen, Camden and Greene counties thirteen each, and Jefferson County twelve. Counties with anywhere from two to eight caves with

The Franz Langendoerfer wine cellar near Hermann, Missouri, situated in a natural cave. The cave opening was simply walled up with rock. The photographer of this 1909 postcard is unknown. (Courtesy Gordon Smith Collection, National Cave Museum, Diamond Caverns, Park City, Kentucky)

springhouse and water supply ruins include Barry, Boone, Crawford, Dent, Jasper, McDonald, Miller, Morgan, Ozark, Perry, Phelps, Ralls, Shannon, Ste. Genevieve, St. Louis, Stone, Webster, Wright, and Texas. There are an additional twelve counties that have one cave each with such evidence.

Ozark caves have also been used as barns for cattle, sheep, goats, and swine. In the 1930s, an eccentric goat herder used a cave in southwestern Missouri as a shelter for both himself and his goats, thus inspiring the name Goat Man Cave.

Pulaski County has six caves that were once used as barns, St. Clair County has four, Phelps County has three, and Iron, Laclede, McDonald, Miller, Ste. Genevieve, and Stone counties have one cave each that served as a barn. Hayes Cave in Stone County has been a natural barn since 1860. In the 1840s, the cave provided a home for the homesteading Prichard family from Tennessee. Subsequent owners of the property used the cave as a barn for more than a hundred years.

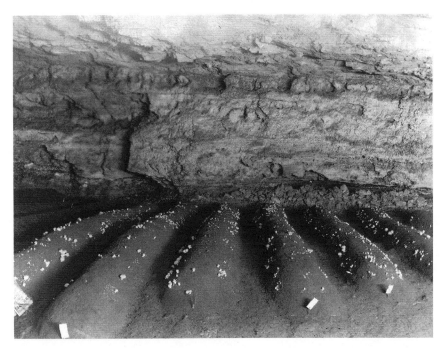

Mushroom beds in Mushroom Cave in Meramec State Park, Franklin County, ca. 1928. (State Historical Society of Missouri, Columbia)

Experimental farming has also occurred in some Ozark caves with attempts at raising celery and rhubarb. Many caves have been used to store watermelons and potatoes. There are eight caves in the Missouri Ozarks named Potato Cave: Christian, Dade, Greene, Miller, Ozark, and Shannon counties have Potato caves. Greene and Webster counties each have a Potato Cellar Cave, and Miller County has a Potato Spring Cave. Eight Missouri caves are named Sweet Potato Cave. Douglas County has three such caves, Texas County has two, and Barry, Miller, and Pulaski counties have one Sweet Potato Cave each. Vernon County has Tater House Cave.

Apples were once commonly stored in Ozark caves. Jacob's Cave in Morgan County was used for apple storage in the 1920s and 1930s. A news item in the *Eldon Advertiser* on October 12, 1933, reported: "The Versailles Orchards Company, operators and owners of one of the largest apple orchards in the state located south of

Versailles, are storing a portion of their crop in Jacob's Cave. . . . About 1,500 bushel baskets have been placed in a part of the cavern and more will be put in later. The cave has a year 'round temperature of about 60 degrees and makes an ideal storage place for fruits."

Although the food most often associated with underground farming in Missouri is mushrooms, only one cave in the Ozarks is named Mushroom Cave as a result of such commercial activity: Mushroom Cave, in Meramec State Park, in Franklin County. Mushroom Cave has three openings. Two openings are a thousand feet apart, but between them is a third opening that is considered the cave's main entrance. Today the cave's entrances are gated to protect an endangered bat colony. The cave has about fourteen hundred feet of spacious passage. In 1899, H. B. Kerriush of Sullivan raised mushrooms in the cave, leading to its name. His first attempt failed to show a profit, but he tried again between 1922 and 1927 with more success, shipping his product in fifty-pound lots to points as distant as Kansas City and Cincinnati, Ohio. When it was time to harvest the crop, trucks could be driven into the cave to the mushroom beds.

In the early 1900s, mushroom farming was carried out in both Crystal Cave and Sequiota Cave in Greene County near Springfield. During the 1930s, mushroom farming took place in Cameron Cave in Cave Hollow just south of Hannibal, and Poole Hollow Cave in Phelps County was the site of a mushroom-farming operation during the early years of the twentieth century. Poole Hollow Cave has an entrance seventy-five feet wide and twelve feet high. A masonry wall was constructed across the entrance to shut out daylight. The cave floor was smoothed out, and horizontal rows of mushroom beds were created for the edible fungi. Trucks reportedly backed into the cave for a distance of eighty yards to pick up the crop when it was harvested.

Mushroom farming in natural caves appears to have been plagued with problems, most associated with efforts to control the setting and protect the crop from fungus, diseases, and critters that like the cave environment. As late as the 1960s, however, people were still considering Ozark caves as sites for mushroom farms. In June 1966 the Missouri Division of Commerce and Industrial Development received a letter requesting information about Missouri caves suitable for such farming. The company requested a list of caves that had ceiling heights of ten feet or greater, at least two hundred feet of overburden (overburden is the amount of soil and rock between the ground surface and the roof of the cave), and a minimum of one hundred thousand square feet of floor space. The letter was referred to the Missouri Geological Survey, which provided an answer listing the square footage of fourteen caves that met the requirements. One of the caves on the list was Mushroom Cave in Meramec State Park. The reply also recommended the use of mines and underground quarries instead of caves, because mines have uniform ceiling heights, level or nearly level floors, and are easily accessible. In the Kansas City area, numerous abandoned underground quarries have been converted into very useful commercial and industrial sites.

Before and even after the arrival of electricity, more than one Ozark dweller came up with the clever idea of piping cave air into his home to provide air conditioning during the hot and sweltering days of summer. Show cave operators had the same idea and began building their gift shops, ticket offices, and administrative headquarters over or within the entrance of their caves. In the 1950s, one enterprising hog farmer in Boone County had the clever notion of piping cool cave air into his hog barns to keep the swine comfortable in summer and avoid the loss of many hogs to extreme heat.

As a means of air conditioning, the scheme of using cave air works, but there are downsides. A home or building cooled with cave air will soon take on the earthy, musty, basementlike smell of the cave. Cave air is humid, and mold can be a persistent problem. Filtering the cave air and using a dehumidifier can help, but most Ozarkers have given up the idea of air conditioning their home with cave air. Several Missouri show caves still air-condition their facilities with cave air, and one of the most successful is Meramec Caverns near Stanton.

These kinds of farm and home uses for Ozark caves have received little attention from historians and the media, but one use for the caves has been widely publicized in the past—their use as locations for moonshine stills during the days of prohibition.

7

Beer and Moonshine

A long time ago . . . there was a little brewery in Zell [Zell Cave], and their product was aged down here. One night a hogshead sprang a leak. It was empty by morning, and all the beer had disappeared down cracks in the floor. About the middle of that forenoon, a German farmer in the valley below, came into town wildly excited. "Mein Gott, Mein Gott!" he cried, "mein schpring, she is running beer!"
—J HARLEN BRETZ, *Caves of Missouri*, 1956

Walter B. Stevens published a history of Missouri's early taverns in 1921 in the *Missouri Historical Review*, reporting: "The oddest tavern in Missouri was not built with hands. It was a cave, forty feet wide and twenty feet high. . . . Boatmen steered their pirogues and longhorns to the bank and took shelter in that cave from the driving storms on the Missouri. They called it 'The Tavern.'"

On May 14, 1804, Lewis and Clark paid a visit to this sandstone shelter cave along the banks of the Missouri River in Franklin County. The cave still exists, though access to it is difficult because of landowner restrictions. The river once lapped at its banks just below the cave but has since retreated some two hundred feet, leaving its flow to deposit enough silt and sand to create a substantial amount of land between the cave and the river. Today, the cave is almost invisible to boatmen, except in winter, because of the cottonwoods that have since grown up on this new landmass.

Above Tavern Rock Cave rises an impressive bluff three hundred feet high. Near the base of the bluff are railroad tracks that pass over

L. S. Huck, the proprietor of Zell Cave and Pop's Tavern, at the far end of his cave, located in Zell, Missouri, in Ste. Genevieve County, in the early 1900s. (Schuster Studio, Hermann, Missouri; courtesy Gordon Smith collection, National Cave Museum, Diamond Caverns, Park City, Kentucky)

the roof of the cave. In fact, when the railroad was built many decades ago, much rock was blasted from the bluff. Some of this waste rock now lies near the cave. It is fortunate that the railroad builders chose not to run the tracks at a lower level. Had they done so, this historic site might have been destroyed.

Captain Lewis recorded: "We passed a large cave on the Lbd. Side called by the French The Tavern—about 120 feet wide 40 feet deep and 20 feet high—many different images are painted on the rock at this place—the Inds. and French pay omage—Many names are wrote on the rock."

Time and weathering of the sandstone has robbed us of these names and images because the interior of the cave is so exposed to the weather. Some recent visitors claim they can still see faint traces of some of the etchings, but the remaining marks are now impossible to interpret. Later explorers, including Zebulon Pike in 1806 and the German Prince Maximilian of Wied in 1833, visited Tavern Rock Cave. Maximilian was quite taken by this site as well as by other "tavern caves" that he learned about during his expedition. Rivers were the highways of travel and commerce in pioneer times. Boatmen, trappers, hunters, and others found riverside caves useful as temporary shelter. The caves were warm in the winter, were cool in the summer, and gave safe retreat from the mosquitoes that inhabited the marshes and sloughs along the river. More than one enterprising Frenchman set up business in these riverside caves, offering trade goods and services of comfort as well as strong drink. Other notable riverside "tavern caves" were found along the banks of the Gasconade and Osage rivers.

Beginning in the early 1820s, when settlers started to filter into southern Missouri and lay claim to fertile bottomlands and natural springs, the distilling of strong drink took place in caves all across the Ozarks. Many immigrants brought distilling skills, especially the settlers from the hills of Kentucky and Tennessee, where the distilling of whiskey had its inception between 1776 and 1793.

In colonial times beer was considered a food product and a healthful stimulant. Alcoholic beverages also had important medicinal and household uses. Men, women, children, and even people of most religious faiths were beer drinkers, and it was not widely considered a public, moral, or religious issue. Today, the drinking of alcoholic beverages is viewed largely as a recreational pursuit and is heavily regulated.

Throughout much of the Old World, there was a greater consumption of beer than water from the 1600s to the 1800s, because pure drinking water was so difficult to find in Europe. But when European and American settlers entered Missouri, they discovered the Ozark hills were watered by countless cold, pure, freshwater springs. It seemed almost too good to be true. Since a great many caves in the Ozarks produce spring-fed streams, springs and caves made ideal locations for the "family recipe." The brewing and distilling of alcoholic beverages in those days was a cottage industry; more often than not, the family still produced only enough beer, wine, or liquor for its own use.

In settlement days, backwoods production of alcoholic beverages depended upon the season of the year, unless a way could be found to secure complete independence from outside temperature variations. So it was that Ozarkians turned to caves; caves were plentiful and maintained a nearly constant temperature every day of the year.

As time passed, the distilling of backwoods liquor spawned an industry because of the need for laborers, craftsmen, boatmen, teamsters, coopers (barrel makers), and farmers—all of them playing some role in the manufacturing, packaging, transportation, and selling of alcoholic beverages. As a consequence, men of greater ambition moved their distilling operations to locations with greater population densities and better transportation facilities. At this time, neither commercial nor private distillers were taxed or licensed by government agencies.

In the 1830s and 1840s, waves of German immigrants began to arrive in Missouri. The influx of German brewers during this period had a huge impact on Missouri culture, especially in the St. Louis area. The first beer in St. Louis was brewed as early as 1810 and sold for ten dollars a barrel. The tax records of 1811 indicate that in that year there was at least one distiller in the city. But by the 1840s, the city's brewers included Stifel and Winkelmeyer, who founded the Union Brewery; the Washington Brewery, established by George Schneider; the Lemp Brewery, established by J. Adam Lemp; and

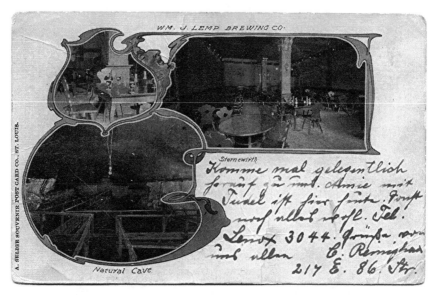

The William J. Lemp Brewing Company of St. Louis used a cave for the storage and cooling of beer. The cave also housed a beer garden where patrons could enjoy a naturally air-conditioned environment. This rare postcard, dated 1921, features three images of the underground facilities. The note, in German, invites a friend to visit. The cave became a show cave in 1945 as Cherokee Cave. Highway construction destroyed a portion of the cave in the late 1960s. (Courtesy Gordon Smith Collection, National Cave Museum, Diamond Caverns, Park City, Kentucky)

the Joseph Uhrig Brewing Company, originally established by Joseph Uhrig and A. Kraut. Others came in the 1850s and 1860s.

What these breweries had in common, besides the production of Missouri's first lager beers, were the caves they used for the cooling and storage of their product. The hills along the west side of the Mississippi River south of the mouth of the Missouri River in the St. Louis area are noted for the presence of sinkholes and caves. The band of topography containing these caves and sinkholes runs south from the city and follows the river all the way to Cape Girardeau. This strip of cavernous terrain is roughly 125 miles long by three miles wide and currently has more than one thousand known caves.

Within the city of St. Louis itself, there are twenty–nine known caves today; however, a great many more cave openings existed in settlement times. Growth of the city over the past two centuries has led to the destruction of many caves and sinkholes as they were filled in and paved over for the construction of buildings, roads, parking lots, and homes. Today, caves within the St. Louis area are largely ignored except in park settings. But from the 1840s to the 1890s, when no electricity was available, they were important resources, especially for brewers. The caves provided natural cooling in a controlled setting, which could be enhanced through modifications of the cave passages and the creation of ice storage chambers.

Some of the more extensive cave systems beneath the city exist only in segments, as long stretches of their passageways are naturally filled with clay, gravel, and other sediments. More than one brewery, some located many city blocks apart, used isolated segments of the same cave system. When necessary, the brewers excavated the sediments to enlarge their portion of the cave. The growth of the brewing industry in St. Louis, and the continued arrival of Germans, spread the industry both south and west of St. Louis. German breweries sprang up in other parts of the state, and some of them used natural caves as well as man-made underground cellars to cool and store their product.

As the nineteenth century wore on, temperance movements arose to do battle with the brewers and the tavern, saloon, and nightclub proprietors who sold the beer. The federal government also began licensing and taxing the manufacturers and retailers of alcoholic beverages. In St. Louis, the legal breweries adapted to these problems with little trouble, but in the hills of the Ozarks, it was a different matter. Many Missouri Ozark natives, clannish, set in their ways, and resentful of any effort by the government to tax their whiskey or regulate their activities, made an even greater effort to hide their stills. Caves, of course, were perfect sites for secretive activities. It was at this time, in the 1880s, that the term *moonshine* came into use, because much of the whiskey making took place at night.

Government tax collectors were faced with a dangerous situation as they began to prowl the back roads and hills of the Ozarks. They followed spring-fed streams to their sources in an effort to locate caves where stills might be operating. They sniffed for the presence

In the 1920s and 1930s, during Prohibition, moonshiners in the Ozarks often used spring-fed cave streams as a source of water for their illegal stills. It was not uncommon for them to hide the still inside a cave to conceal the operation from neighbors and law enforcement officers. (Lyons Memorial Library, College of the Ozarks)

of smoke and mash. But they were in enemy territory where the tight-lipped population consisted of many intermarried families. And most Ozarkers went armed and were quite willing to defend their property against intrusion by government snoopers. The problem worsened as the tax kept rising. By 1894, the government was demanding a tax of $1.10 per gallon, which, by the standards of Ozark living, was considered outrageous.

And then the Eighteenth Amendment to the U.S. Constitution, which went into effect on January 16, 1920, brought nationwide prohibition and led to one of the most lawless periods in American history. The law criminalized the production and selling of alcoholic beverages. Although the rate of criminal activity in the state was the highest in St. Louis, out in the hills and hollows of the Ozarks, the stills went deeper underground and grew even more numerous following the stock market crash in 1929, which brought tough financial times even to the hill country. We have no way of knowing exactly how many or what caves in the Ozarks provided cover for moonshine stills, because the caves were often unnamed and the moonshiners did not keep records of their illegal activities. Missouri Supreme Court and circuit court case files, however, contain a wealth of information about this period of illegal moonshining in the Ozark hills, and Ozark folklore is riddled with moonshine stories.

Records of the Missouri Speleological Survey list more than forty caves scattered across twenty-three Missouri counties that have a surviving story or some physical evidence associated with legal brewing or illegal moonshine activities. Excluding St. Louis County and the City of St. Louis, most of these counties are in the Ozark region. Christian County has five such caves. Barry, Perry, and Shannon counties have three each, while Boone, Benton, Camden, and Taney counties have two caves each. Sixteen caves in the state have one of the following words as the first or primary word in their name: Moonshine, Whiskey, Still, Beer, Bootlegger, and Brewery.

Times have changed, and whiskey making in the caves of the Ozarks appears to be a colorful cottage industry of the past. Today, it seems, cave enthusiasts who venture into the Ozark hills have more to fear from the guardians of methamphetamine labs, marijuana growers, and black-market artifact hunters than from the guardians of moonshine stills.

But there was a time when Civil War guerrillas used Ozark caves as hideouts, and outlaws of the Reconstruction years also took refuge in the caves. The outlaws of the 1870s and later were such a problem in the Ozarks that for a time people called Missouri "the Outlaw State."

8

War and Outlaws

Local authorities claim the ubiquitous James boys used the cave
[James Brothers Cave, Jackson County] for a hideaway. The
boys would appear, considering all the claims of this kind, to
have been Missouri's first and most active spelunkers.
—J HARLEN BRETZ, *Caves of Missouri*, 1956

While many Missouri caves were put to benign and beneficial
uses in the nineteenth and twentieth centuries, some caves
served the needs of criminals, Civil War guerrillas, Reconstruction-
period outlaws, and hate groups. Civil defense and military authorities have also left footprints on the pages of Missouri cave history. It
began early.

Honest, law-abiding immigrants were not alone as they crossed
the Mississippi River and made their way into the Ozarks in the
1830s. The criminal element came along, too. One group of criminals chose to settle in the shadowy dells of a geologically unusual
place that would later be known as Ha Ha Tonka in Camden County.

A man named Garland came to Ha Ha Tonka first. He built a
gristmill and dammed the flow of Ha Ha Tonka Spring in 1830.
Legend holds that he was the front man for outlaws and that the
gristmill operation was simply to cover future criminal activities.
There are many unknowns in this troubled period in the history of
Ha Ha Tonka. It may be that the outlaws and counterfeiters who
hunkered down here in 1831 came from Cave-in-Rock along the
Ohio River or had close ties to the criminal dynasty that inhabited
that locale for many years.

Entrance to Counterfeiters' Cave at Ha Ha Tonka State Park in Camden County, where counterfeiters and other outlaws made their headquarters in the 1830s. (Postcard by Manchester, Manchester Studio, Lebanon, Missouri, ca. 1915, from the author's collection)

Cave-in-Rock is a cave in a bluff at the southern tip of Illinois along the Ohio River about eighty miles east of Cape Girardeau, Missouri, where nineteenth-century river pirates and counterfeiters operated for many years, preying upon traffic that came down the Ohio. They left a bloody history in the Cave-in-Rock area.

Among the outlaws at Cave-in-Rock was a man named Sturdevant, who became a notorious and successful counterfeiter during the settlement period. He was an artist at his illegal trade, an engraver of unequaled skill. He was also ruthless and headed a network of counterfeiting operations throughout the western country. He had rules for his talented subordinates—they were not allowed to pass counterfeit bank notes and coins in the area or state in which they operated, and they were to surround themselves with loyal criminals who would defend them and cover their counterfeiting activities.

When the criminals had to flee Cave-in-Rock country, Sturdevant disappeared. What became of him is not known, but there is reason

Tales of Jesse James pervade Missouri folklore. Even though oral history places him in numerous caves throughout the Ozarks, only two caves are currently called Jesse James Cave. One of these caves is in Perry County and the other is in Vernon County. Cliff Cave, in Cliff Cave Park in St. Louis County, was known as Jesse James Cave in the early 1900s. This postcard, ca. 1920, shows men standing at the cave entrance, beside the ruins of the Cliff Cave Wine Company, which used the cave in the late 1800s. (Courtesy Gordon Smith Collection, National Cave Museum, Diamond Caverns, Park City, Kentucky)

to believe that he might have been at Ha Ha Tonka for a time or that the gang located there was an extension of his counterfeiting network. When the gang set up shop in several caves at Ha Ha Tonka, they brought with them skillfully engraved plates, presses, and molds. They set about manufacturing high-quality Mexican, Canadian, and American coins and bank notes, just as Sturdevant had been doing in the Cave-in-Rock area. The Ha Ha Tonka counterfeiters did not circulate the money in their area. Reportedly, they shipped the fake currency down the Osage River to the Missouri River to be taken elsewhere.

Unfortunately for the counterfeiters, the criminal element they depended upon for protection committed too many local crimes. The law-abiding settlers organized a "vigilance committee" with enforcers known as "the Slickers." When a suspect outlaw was caught, he was tied to a tree, whipped severely, and ordered to leave the area. The technique backfired because the outlaws organized an "Anti-Slicker" force, and in the late 1830s the Niangua and Osage river valleys became embroiled in the Slicker War.

It was a violent and fearful time that led to several deaths. The war did not end until after the county was organized in 1841 as Kinderhook County, a name changed soon afterward to Camden County. Organization of the county government brought the Ha Ha Tonka area into the county's jurisdiction, making it possible for local, state, and federal authorities to join forces and put an end to the outlaw operation.

The Slicker War was but a prelude to a bloodier conflict that erupted in the 1850s along the Missouri-Kansas border, a fight between proslavery and abolitionist settlers on both sides of the state boundary. The hate spawned by this prelude to the Civil War gave birth to outlaw gangs that would bathe Missouri in blood well through the 1870s. Chief among the outlaws were Jesse James, Cole Younger, and their followers and imitators.

The Civil War itself was destined to leave a legacy of folklore surrounding Missouri caves. Scores of caves in the Ozarks are at the center of legends and tales about men who hid out in the caves to avoid conscription, of families and small villages that hid their valuables in caves to keep them safe from guerrilla raids, and of Union and Confederate forces that used caves for the storage of munitions and other supplies.

After the Confederate victory at the Battle of Wilson's Creek in 1861 and later defeat at Pea Ridge, the larger forces of the Confederacy were kept out of Missouri by Federal troops. Federal patrols controlled the major rivers and roads of the state, but insurgents and Confederate sympathizers controlled the backwoods. Bands of guerrillas roamed the hills. Many of their rendezvous points were at caves, and a network of cave hideouts made it possible for them to have a nearly free run of the Ozark region.

Among the more notorious guerrillas that haunted the regions of central Missouri where caves are numerous—along the Gasconade and Big and Little Piney rivers—were secessionist "General Crabtree," Bill Wilson, Jim Jamison, Anthony Wright, and Dick Kitchen.

Secessionist Crabtree came north at the beginning of the war, reportedly to recruit Cole and Miller county men to fight for the Southern cause. To the displeasure of Miller County residents, he stayed in the area to raid, making his headquarters in caves, moving frequently from cave to cave to avoid Federal patrols. Crabtree eluded capture due largely to his network of cave hideouts but met his end in August 1864 when he received a fatal wound. He managed to get back to his cave home, where a woman he had been living with was waiting. Though his enemies pursued him, he was left to die in the arms of the woman, who claimed to be his lawful wife. He was buried nearby in an unmarked grave in Cole County. The cave in which he died is known to this day as Crabtree Cave.

East of Miller County along the Little and Big Piney rivers, Bill Wilson and his guerrilla band were carrying out their own backwoods vendettas against Federal patrols. They also engaged in a great deal of looting and burning of homes and barns. Caves known to have been important links in Wilson's escape routes after bloody encounters with soldiers included Huffman Cave, Gourd Creek Cave, Renaud Cave, and Point Bluff Cave, all in Phelps County. After the war, Bill Wilson and most of his bushwhacking buddies fled central Missouri, and Wilson himself was never heard from again.

The Civil War left many areas of the Ozarks in chaos. Into this bitter state of affairs rode the James Gang, the Youngers, and a host of

Youngers' Cave is one of the several caves in a bluff along the Osage River at Monegaw Springs in St. Clair County. The cave was named for the Younger Gang, who frequented the locale in the 1870s. (Becraft Photo, ca. 1910; from the author's collection)

lesser outlaws. They robbed banks and railroads and created such havoc that, for a time, Missouri was called "the Outlaw State." Some people scoff at the many tales, traditions, and legends that associate Jesse James with Missouri caves. Time erases documentation, and legends grow as the years increase.

Victims of the crime sprees perpetrated by the outlaws were never sure what outlaw was riding with whom at the time of a robbery. Imagination and the inability to identify Jesse James resulted in many erroneous stories. Some tales placed Jesse James pulling robberies in two different states at the same time. And it is quite possible that when members of these outlaw gangs were spotted in remote Ozark locales, people just assumed they were using a local cave as a hideout. So cave hideout stories multiplied.

When the show cave industry sprang up in the Ozarks in the 1880s and 1890s, the Jesse James saga was still a hot topic of conversation even though Jesse was killed in 1882. Show cave developers began to promote their own outlaw legends to add mystery and suspense to the history of their attraction. The one show cave that has bested all the others in advancing its Jesse James legend is Meramec Caverns near Stanton.

Cave names lead us to many of these stories that hark back to the days of the Civil War and the turbulent outlaw years that followed. There are three caves called Civil War Cave, one each in Camden, Christian, and Vernon counties. Perry and Polk counties both have an Ambush Cave. The Baldknobbers, a much-feared vigilante group in the Taney County area between 1865 and 1884, have a cluster of caves in Christian, Stone, and Taney counties named for them. There is one cave in Stone County called Belle Starr Cave and two Outlaw caves, one each in Franklin and Phelps counties. Belle Starr was known in southwest Missouri as "the Bandit Queen"; from 1875 to 1880, she led a band of cattle and horse thieves. Benton County has a Bushwhacker Cave, as do Pulaski and Texas counties. Vernon County just happens to have four caves named Bushwhacker, as well as a Quantrill Cave, named for the Confederate guerrilla William Clarke Quantrill.

Shannon County has a Peter Renfro Cave. Peter Renfro was a villain that most Missourians of today have never heard of, but in the 1880s and 1890s, his name was on the lips of just about everybody who lived in southern Missouri. In July 1888, Renfro killed Constable Charles Dorris during a brawl at a picnic in Summerville, along the Shannon-Texas county line, and then fled into the hills. All efforts to find him failed. It was rumored he had left the state. But then a new rumor surfaced, suggesting that he was hiding in a cave not far from his home. A search was made and the cave was located, but the cave entrance was down on the face of a cliff and could only be approached by descent from above—which was considered suicide. The cave reportedly had other entrances, but law officers could not find them. The officers were also unable to catch the person or persons said to be getting food to Renfro.

Renfro was captured at the cave about a year later. He was confined to the Springfield jail for two years, tried for murder, convicted, and sentenced to hang. But a week before the sentence was to be carried out, he escaped by overpowering his jailer and taking the keys from him. Peter Renfro disappeared again, but this time he covered his tracks so well that no one could find him.

In 1893 a newspaper article appeared describing his cave hideout. The newspaper reporter, who would not reveal the location of Renfro's cave, said Renfro was constantly armed and had a faithful, well-trained watchdog. Renfro might have escaped capture for a decade or more if he had chosen to remain an underground recluse, but he didn't. In February 1898, five years later, he was captured at the old Doniphan Club House in upper Ripley County. Judge McAfee of the Greene County criminal court resentenced Renfro to be hanged, but a petition circulated in southern Missouri, pleading for the governor to commute Renfro's sentence to life in prison. On May 12, 1898, Missouri governor Lon V. Stephens granted the request and Renfro spent his last years in the state penitentiary at Jefferson City.

Between 1915 and 1925, caves in Greene, Jasper, and Newton counties became the meeting places for the Ku Klux Klan (KKK), a secret fraternal group that confined its membership to American-born white Protestants; it was originally formed to maintain white supremacy and later opposed immigrants and non-Protestant religious groups. In 1924, the Springfield Klan purchased Knox Cave northwest of the city, which was the site of an underground nightclub. For six years, the Klan used the cave as a "temple." Unable to meet mortgage payments, the Klan eventually lost the cave, which later became a show cave under the name Temple Caverns. Today, it is called Fantastic Caverns.

In Newton County the Klan made use of Jolly Cave in the upper reaches of Capps Creek near its junction with Shoal Creek in the eastern part of the county. Jolly Cave is essentially one large room about 200 feet long, 40 to 60 feet wide, and 10 to 20 feet high with a nearly level, hard-packed clay floor. It is said that when the KKK used the cave, they would lead their horses down into the cave and stable them there. How long the KKK used the cave is currently unknown. The use of caves by the Ku Klux Klan seems to have been a phenomenon only of the 1920s, when the Klan experienced a short rebirth nationwide.

Events of World War II and the emergence of the Cold War

between the United States and the Soviet Union again turned attention to the possibilities of Missouri caves. In the late 1940s, the U.S. Navy surveyed some three hundred caves within a fifty-mile radius of Rolla, Missouri, looking for one suitable to house a jet propulsion laboratory. The navy's project, called "Project Cavern," was a military secret for many years. This 1951 project was carried out by a U.S. Naval Reserve attachment at Rolla, Missouri. An early report on Project Cavern produced by the Office of Naval Research was published in *Missouri Speleology,* the journal of the Missouri Speleological Survey (MSS), in 2005.

In the early 1960s, Missouri civil defense authorities came to the MSS requesting information and locations for Missouri caves. They wanted to see how many caves might be usable as fallout shelters, where people could go for protection in the event of a nuclear attack. The Missouri Civil Defense Agency in Jefferson City eventually released the "Mine and Cave Fallout Shelter Survey," which listed 212 wild caves scattered across thirty-eight Missouri counties. They were caves that had at least one thousand square feet of floor space that might be suitable for the agency's purposes.

Fortunately, neither the owners of the wild caves nor civil defense authorities rushed out to convert the caves into actual fallout shelters, which could have resulted in irreparable damage to many caves. The caves did, however, receive official designation with metal Fallout Shelter signs posted near their entrances listing each cave's holding capacity (the number of people the cave could accommodate in an emergency).

For Missouri show cave operators it was a different matter entirely. They leaped to the cause, seeing it as an opportunity for free publicity. A news release published in the *Reveille* newspaper at Camdenton, on November 14, 1961, reported that the Missouri Caves Association assisted the state civil defense director, Dean Lupkey, in setting up an advisory committee on the use of caves as fallout shelters. Eddie Miller, manager of Bridal Cave, served as chairman, with committee members Bob Hudson of Meramec Caverns, Waldo Powell of Fairy Cave, and Ohle Ohlson of Ozark Caverns.

The show caves reaped tons of publicity with the issue and were still benefiting from Cold War scares as late as 1969 when civil defense supplies were still being stashed away in various show caves throughout the state.

Murders, thieves, counterfeiters, guerrillas, and hooded hoodlums have come and gone in the darkness of Missouri caves. They accomplished little other than leaving a legacy of legends that have perpetuated their names and the memory of their unsavory behavior. Even the designs of well-meaning military authorities and civil defense officials came to naught when they turned their attention to the caves of Missouri. The caves survived largely intact and undamaged by the plans and activities of these agents, but many caves in the Ozarks did not fare so well when they caught the attention of onyx miners during the late nineteenth century.

9

Onyx Mining

For several years the attention of scientists and lapi-
daries has been attracted to the wonderful deposits of
onyx in Central Missouri. The residents in the neighborhood of the caves and the owners of the land upon
which they are located, until very recently, did not
know and appreciate the value of the wealth stored in
them.
—*New Era* newspaper, March 14, 1891

"Throughout the Ozark region there are caves in the dolomite
and limestone formations . . . filled in whole or in part with
travertine, or cave onyx, as it is called. This onyx resembles the
Mexican variety and often, when polished, exhibits beautiful surfaces,
having a variegated coloring," wrote state geologist Henry A. Buehler
in *The Biennial Report of the State Geologist,* published by the Missouri
Bureau of Geology and Mines in 1906. "But," Buehler noted, "it is seldom obtainable in large blocks free from flaws, for which reason
attempts to exploit these deposits have been abandoned."

In the late 1800s and early 1900s, polished marble was much in
demand throughout the world for ornamental and decorative interior and exterior architectural work. The stone was used for many
purposes, including flooring, mantels, paneling, clock cases, lamp
bases, tabletops, washbasins, statuary, vases, and columns. It was
commonly used in public buildings and luxury homes.

In the stone trade, the term *marble* is applied to any rock containing
large amounts of calcium carbonate that is capable of taking a good

polish and is suitable for ornamental work or high-grade construction. For commercial use, the rock must have a desirable color, be able to be quarried in blocks of large size free from cracks or impure layers, and have a fine texture.

The most suitable stone for this purpose is crystalline limestone and dolomite, which formed as sediment in shallow waters of inland seas between 100 and 500 million years ago. These rocks are generally composed of more than 50 percent carbonate minerals, which were derived from the skeletons and shells of ancient sea life that died and settled to the bottom of the seas. There is a great range in color, the most common being variations and mixtures of gray, white, black, yellow, pink, and green. The colors are largely due to impurities that give the stone a "banded" or "grained" appearance.

Beds of marble occur in many geologic formations. Because marble comes in such variety and from so many parts of the world, it is a stone of many names. But among these names are certain ones that have a special meaning to jewelers and craftsmen, and which were especially popular in the closing years of the nineteenth century. These terms are *onyx, cave onyx, onyx marble, Mexican onyx, black onyx,* and *travertine.*

Onyx marble and *onyx* differ somewhat from marbles of the common type. Marbles commonly used in high-grade construction are from bedrock layers of limestone and dolomite. But onyx marble and onyx are essentially crystalline deposits derived from the dissolving and breaking down of limestone and dolomite by groundwater. Onyx marbles form in one of two ways—as the product of hot springwater deposits that develop on the surface at a spring outlet, or as deposits left by cold, mineral-laden drip water in caves. The deposits formed by hot springs are generally called *travertine* or *tufa,* such as the famous travertine or tufa deposits in Yellowstone National Park. The deposits left by drip water in caves takes the form of stalactites, stalagmites, columns, and flowstone on the floors, walls, and ceiling of limestone caverns. It is the cold-water deposits that are generally called *cave onyx* or *onyx.* The term *black onyx* refers to a form of onyx marble that is pure black. *Mexican onyx* is largely a form of travertine or onyx marble that is quarried and processed in Mexico.

Scar left by onyx miners in a Pulaski County cave in the early 1900s. Later cave explorers added insult to injury by putting graffiti on the cave's formations and walls. The rock pick has nothing to do with the mining; it was added for scale when the photo was taken. (Photo by H. Dwight Weaver, 1959)

Since the late 1800s, much of the world's finest onyx marble has been produced by Mexico. At most quarry sites, this stone has been of the banded travertine variety, but some had originally formed in caves that later had their walls and roofs destroyed by erosion, leaving the cave onyx deposits on the surface. Cave onyx and other onyx marbles were first brought to the attention of architects, sculptors, and builders in 1862, when the French made a large, beautiful display with it at the International Exhibition of London. The exhibit was fashioned from stalagmite formations found in Algiers. Onyx was also displayed at later expositions, including the World's Columbian Exposition in Chicago in 1893 and the St. Louis World's Fair in 1904.

In the late 1880s, mining entrepreneurs in the United States began searching for deposits of cave onyx in the caves of Kentucky, Tennessee, and Missouri. These states are noted for having many caves formed in limestone and dolomite, caves adorned with formations composed of cave onyx. By December 1890, the *St. Louis Globe-Democrat* newspaper was promoting the discoveries of prospectors who wanted to exploit local cave onyx deposits. These speculators, the paper said in headlines, had found "miles of subterranean wonders—onyx of all colors and immeasurable extent—great chambers lined with the beautiful stone." The best deposits, according to the reports, were found in caves in Crawford and Pulaski counties, Missouri. "Millions in Onyx" said at least one newspaper headline in 1891. This article went on to report that a company had been formed in St. Louis to work the deposits in Crawford and Pulaski counties.

"Experts from different parts of the country were secured and all the caves in Pulaski and Crawford counties . . . were inspected," the *New Era* newspaper reported in March 1891. "The result of the investigation satisfied the members of the syndicate that they had come into possession of a veritable bonanza. Onyx was found in nearly all of the caves, but only in small quantities in most of them. The main formation seemed to be in three caves and four open workings." Two of the caves and quarries were located in Crawford County, and one cave and two quarries in Pulaski County, according to the paper. The unnamed cave in Pulaski County was Onyx Cave, about five miles northeast of St. Robert. This cave was sometimes called Boiling Springs Cave. In the 1990s, it was a show cave, operated as Onyx Mountain Caverns.

The surface quarries in Missouri that contained onyx deposits were, in the language of that day, "broken down caves," or in other words, very ancient caves that had been unroofed and destroyed by surface erosion.

Onyx mining began at Onyx Mountain Caverns in 1892. The stone was destined for use in the St. Louis Post-Dispatch building in St. Louis and at other sites. Work started with the sinking of a deep shaft, eight feet by thirteen feet, to reach the deposits that were located nearly a thousand feet into the cave from its natural entrance. The shaft penetrated eight feet of soil and loose rock and then ninety-two feet of solid rock before entering the cave. A substantial amount of onyx was removed from the cave chamber at the bottom of the shaft, as well as from a nearly onyx-filled passage that leads from the shaft chamber back toward the cave's natural entrance. Work at the cave continued until it became apparent that much of the stone removed from the cave was commercially unusable. It was riddled with minute fissures that caused the stone to break apart when being cut and shaped at the finishing plant in St. Louis. While suitable for carved figurines and similar small souvenirs, it was unsuitable for projects that required large slabs or blocks of stone.

George P. Merrill, the curator of the Department of Geology at the U.S. National Museum, was the leading authority on onyx marbles in the 1890s. In an 1895 report on the cave onyx mining industry, he stated that there were some disastrous cave onyx mining failures during this period. He attributed it to the incompetence of those who evaluated the volume and quality of the onyx deposits, to the incompetence of the miners who used explosives (which weakened the stone), and to promoters of the industry who had unrealistic expectations.

It became apparent in the decades that followed that most Missouri cave onyx was too flawed for use in construction due to interruptions in the way its layers were deposited over geologic time. But knowledge, wisdom, and experience were apparently in short supply among the cave onyx miners of Missouri from the 1890s to the 1920s. Most had probably never heard of George P. Merrill or read his reports. Most of them had probably not even consulted Missouri's own state geologist, Henry A. Buehler.

The mining at Onyx Mountain Caverns encouraged other onyx mining ventures. By the mid-1890s it was known that the World's Fair was going to be held in St. Louis in 1904. Speculators were sure that architects planning the Missouri buildings for the fair would want cave onyx for decorative uses. Mining entrepreneurs went hunting for caves with suitable deposits of onyx to quarry. By 1893, several caves in Camden County were the focus of onyx mining activities. These caves included King's Onyx Cave and several small adjacent caves near the vanished town of Barnumton, which were totally stripped of their deposits. By 1897 Onyx Cave, along the Big Niangua River about 16.5 miles above its confluence with the Osage River, was also being mined. Today, the waters of the Lake of the Ozarks inundate the onyx-mined portions of this cave.

Big Onyx Cave in Crawford County was subjected to so much blasting that it became unstable, and portions of the cave collapsed. Not far away, in the same county, was Onondaga Cave, where an abortive attempt was also made at mining onyx. In the 1890s, a man named Brown quarried onyx in Onyx Cave about eighteen miles from West Plains in Howell County, reportedly removing thirty tons. Thirty-six years later, in 1928, his son considered reestablishing the onyx mining operation but was apparently persuaded not to do so after a geologist from the Missouri Bureau of Geology and Mines evaluated the site.

By 1901, contractors for the World's Fair announced that they wanted Missouri cave onyx to exhibit in the Mining and Mineralogy Hall and possibly for some of the buildings to be erected. Spurred by this, two engineering students at the Missouri School of Mines and Metallurgy—Ignatius J. Stauber and Fred R. Koeberlin—visited Onyx Mountain Caverns to study the cave's geology and reevaluate its onyx deposits. The bulk of their twenty-four-page thesis was devoted to the possibilities of reopening the mine. In their final analysis, Stauber and Koeberlin were not encouraging about the prospects of reopening the mine. Their concluding paragraph stated: "It should be born in mind however, that there is a great element of uncertainty in working deposits of this kind, as they are rarely uniform for any great distance either in texture or color and the enterprise necessarily partakes of the nature of a lottery." The cave mine was never reopened.

In February 1911, the Missouri State Capitol building in Jefferson City burned. A temporary capitol building was quickly erected nearby and preparations began for the construction of a new permanent capitol building. This also spurred new onyx mining ventures. The Onyx Quarries Company of Boonville filed its corporate papers in 1919 and began development of a mining operation at Arnhold Onyx Cave along the Niangua River in Camden County. This company, too, was destined to fold before removing substantial amounts of onyx. Today, this cave is inundated by the Lake of the Ozarks.

Cave onyx mining speculation continued into the 1930s in Missouri, but by the early 1920s the industry had become all but extinct in the state. Missouri cave onyx producers could not compete with the high quality, low-priced onyx marbles being marketed nationwide by companies in Arizona and California. The mining of onyx from caves in the United States was a short-lived industry that thrived from about 1890 to 1920 in Missouri, Kentucky, and Tennessee. The booming industry was lively and generated boastful newspaper headlines full of speculation and exaggeration. It led to some disastrous financial failures and irreparable damage to a number of beautifully decorated caves.

The history of the onyx mining industry in Missouri's past makes an interesting statement about the attitude of society toward caves during the 1890s and early 1900s. During this period, large segments of society considered caves to be worthless unless they contained some substance of commercial value or could be used for recreation. We are fortunate that the onyx mining industry folded before it was able to damage and destroy more caves than it did, because the miners focused their attention on those caves that were the most beautifully adorned by nature.

Another group of miners who went looking for caves during this same period in Missouri history were seeking a different kind of resource, one that was less solid and more squalid—bat guano. They too had visions of wealth dancing in their heads.

10

Guano Mining

The local wise men all laughed at Weekly when he began his
operations [bat guano mining], and were much chagrined when
they learned that he had sold the first shipment for $500.
—VANCE RANDOLPH, "Cave Bats and a Unique Industry,"
Missouri Magazine, August 1934

"Some months ago a large cave was discovered in Stone County.
. . . A company was organized to develop its varied stores of
wealth in the shape of marble, fuller's earth, etc. but little was said
of the real wealth, which covered the floor . . . to a depth of several
feet. That was kept in the background, and the widely published stories of the cave attracted but little attention," reported the *Current
Wave* newspaper on October 1, 1884. The deposits were later ana-
lyzed and found to be bat guano, which the newspaper called "the
richest guano on the globe, surpassing the famous Peruvian beds,
from which the world has drawn its supplies for more than half a
century."

As soon as the public learned that the guano was valuable, the
news created great excitement in southwest Missouri. Prospectors
went hunting for caves with similar deposits of guano. As a consequence, numerous guano mines were established in caves in Stone
and Christian counties. "Shipments are being made daily to the mar-
kets of the east where it commands a high figure for fertilizing purposes," reported the newspaper. "Prospecting parties are out in
every direction, and it is safe to say that every hill and hollow of
Stone, Christian, Taney and Ozark counties will be more thoroughly

explored than they ever were before, and that every hole will be investigated."

Saltpeter miners had been the first to go looking for deposits of bat guano in Ozark caves, because saltpeter, one of the principal ingredients in gunpowder produced in the early 1800s, can be leached from aging guano. But later, bat guano was sought for its fertilizer value.

Fresh bat guano is black. It has a high moisture content, much nitrogen, and appreciable amounts of phosphorous and potassium—the desirable elements for fertilizers. With age, the guano loses moisture and becomes a dark brown. Very old bat guano can be reddish, pale brown, or gray and becomes quite dusty, unless it is in a cave area where it is subjected to large amounts of dripping water or is periodically inundated by a flooding cave stream.

The chemistry of the bat guano changes as it ages, and the nitrogen changes into ammonia and nitrate. In some instances, bat guano can saturate the cave air with ammonia fumes to a degree that breathing the air becomes dangerous. C. L. Weekly, who mined bat guano from Gentry Cave near Galena, Missouri, in the 1930s, acknowledged this hazard in guano mining. He said he had been forced to abandon some of his guano sites because the cave passages were small and the ammonia fumes were too strong.

The large, unidentified cave mentioned in the 1884 *Current Wave* article was Marvel Cave in Stone County. Ronald L. Martin, in the *Official Guide to Marvel Cave: Its Discovery and Exploration,* first published in 1974, documented the guano mining activities that occurred in this large, deep, spectacular Ozark cave. The mining enterprise began in 1884 and lasted until about 1888. The operation must have been an impressive enterprise in the Ozark hills of that day, because the guano had to be brought to the surface in buckets from a depth of more than a hundred feet. The piles of guano in the great, domed entrance chamber of the cave were twenty-five feet deep. At that time, the market value of the guano, after processing, was seven hundred dollars per ton.

Guano is generally considered to be the manure of seabirds such as pelicans, cormorants, and penguins. Bats are mammals, not birds, but at some early date the word *guano* became associated with the manure of bats, and the term has been used ever since. The islands off the coast of Peru have long been the chief source of supply for guano used as fertilizer around the world, but the guano mining that occurred at Carlsbad Caverns in New Mexico from 1903 to 1923 is one of the best-known former guano mining enterprises in the United States. Carlsbad Caverns is one of America's most popular show caves. Millions of people have toured the cave since 1925 and learned about this episode in the cave's history when more than a hundred thousand tons of guano were removed from the cave.

In 1921, the University of Missouri College of Agriculture released a study by William A. Albrecht (bulletin 180) titled "Bat Guano and Its Fertilizing Value." "The high cost of manufactured fertilizers and the shortage of nitrogenous materials, together with transportation troubles of the past few years, have put precarious conditions about the farmer dependent on commercial fertilizer," said Albrecht. The report went on to mention the various kinds of fertilizers that the farmers would have to resort to using and then encouraged the use of bat guano. "Bat guano . . . should have attention for its possibilities in this respect . . . since caves with bats inhabiting them are common in Missouri."

Albrecht's report concluded, "Average bat guano makes a good fertilizer on poor soils when applied directly at the rate of two hundreds pounds of dry material per acre. As a general fertilizing material it can be used more satisfactorily as a constituent of mixed fertilizer, especially when mixed with phosphorus carriers."

In 1883–1884, a financial panic and depression overtook the nation. It was particularly hard on farmers. This was the economic situation in 1884 when guano mining began in southern Missouri. But the industry seems to have not survived much beyond 1890. During the Great Depression of the 1930s, there was another period of sporadic guano mining in the Ozarks, but the price commanded in 1884—seven hundred dollars per ton—fell to thirty to forty dollars per ton in the mid-1930s.

Missouri's most noteworthy guano miner of the 1930s was C. L. Weekly of Stone County, who mined Gentry Cave along the James River. Gentry Cave has several doorwaylike openings beneath a rock shelter in a bluff. The cave is extensive, with a maze of intersecting

C. L. Weekly (center) and his helpers, with sacks of dried bat guano taken from Gentry Cave in Stone County. (From *Missouri: The Official Publication of the Missouri State Chamber of Commerce,* 1934; courtesy Missouri State Library)

passageways, some of crawling height only. When C. L. Weekly, a wiry, sharp-eyed man of small stature, worked the cave, he was known locally as the "Bat Manure Man." He maintained that the guano he mined, processed, and sold was the best fertilizer in the world. "All the greenhouses use it. . . . I ship mine to Springfield and Kansas City and St. Louis, mostly. Get $35 a ton for it," he told folklorist Vance Randolph in 1934. Upon being taken to a place in the cave where Weekly was working, Randolph noted that the guano deposits were five feet deep, dark brown, perfectly dry, and odorless.

When Weekly took his first shipment of guano to the railroad station and asked for freight-rates on the product, the man at the station thought he was crazy and had difficulty finding the proper rate, because he didn't know what kind of animal a bat was. A nearby loafer, overhearing the conversation, cried out, "My Gosh! Thar ain't bats enough in th' world to make a carload o' th' dang stuff!" Weekly soon proved him wrong.

Weekly and his two helpers wore caps with oil lamps, much like coal miners of that day. They shoveled the guano into big buckets and then carried the buckets to the cave entrance where the guano was spread out on the ground and left to dry. After the guano was dry, it was sifted through wire gravel-screens to remove fragments of rock and other undesirable material. Once sifted, it was put into hundred-pound sacks. Each sack carried a registration tag with a guaranteed chemical analysis, as was required by state law. Weekly's first shipment consisted of 380 hundred-pound sacks, for which he was paid five hundred dollars. That was a handsome sum for Depression days in the Ozarks.

There were hazards to guano mining besides ammonia fumes. At some stages, some guano can be explosive, so using a lamp with a live flame is a hazard. Histoplasmosis, an infectious lung disease, can be contracted by inhaling dusty bat guano that contains spores of the histoplasmosis fungus. Bats themselves do not transmit the disease, but dusty bat guano is a suitable medium for development of the airborne spores of the fungus. It is highly unlikely that C. L. Weekly and his helpers used breathing masks while digging in the guano deposits, which, according to Randolph, were dry and probably quite dusty. Whether or not any of them contracted the lung disease is unknown.

Weekly said only one kind of bat used Gentry Cave. He probably did not know the species, but it was most likely the gray bat. He was also dismayed with the way bats were treated. "Many farmer boys seem to hate bats for some reason," he said, "and sometimes make big wooden paddles and go into the caves where they kill bats by the hundreds."

Missouri "currently provides habitat for eleven species of bats; in addition, four other species of bats have been observed here or may occur here," according to William R. Elliott, cave biologist at the Missouri Department of Conservation. These bats feed exclusively on flying insects. Six of these species spend all or at least part of the year roosting in caves. Only the gray and Indiana bats leave large piles of guano in the caves—the gray bat, in particular, because it not only hibernates in the caves during the winter, but also uses caves as a nursery for rearing young.

Missouri law now protects bats. The Indiana and gray bats are also on the federal Endangered Species List and are thus given special protection. Some of the caves that harbor the largest colonies of gray and Indiana bats in the state are gated. The gates that are installed on bat cave entrances are of a special design that prevents human access yet allows the bats to fly in and out of the cave without harm or impediment. Bats are very particular about the kind of opening through which they will fly. Most bat gates are funded and installed by federal and state agencies, often with the assistance of organized caving groups. Some of Missouri's organized caving groups have also funded the installation of bat gates. Occasionally, a private cave owner will finance such a gate for his cave but rely upon agencies and cavers to do the installation and often the maintenance. Access to these caves is not permitted when the bats are in residence, which means that exploration of the bat caves is possible for only a few weeks or months out of the year.

Only about a hundred of Missouri's 6,200 recorded caves are suitable to gray and Indiana bats for hibernation and rearing their young. The limited number of usable caves, the increasing use of pesticides to control insects, an ever-increasing loss of habitat, and human disturbance have caused a serious decline in the population of these bats over the decades. Saltpeter mining during the settlement period and the guano mining that came later undoubtedly had an impact upon the bats that used the mined caves. Fortunately for the bats, the development of synthetic nitrates eliminated the need to mine saltpeter from caves to manufacture gunpowder and guano for the making of fertilizers.

It has only been during the latter half of the twentieth century that we have learned how truly useful bats can be. They consume enormous quantities of harmful flying insects. And it has only been in recent decades that Missouri has been able to create laws and develop and fund state agency programs designed to protect bats and the caves they use. Public education has progressed considerably since the days when the farmer boys of C. L. Weekly's neighborhood went into caves to kill bats. It still happens occasionally, but today bats are more highly regarded than at any other time in recorded Western history.

The guano miners dug into many unsavory piles of bat manure, but in general they did not disturb the caves in a major way, and the substance they sought actually existed and had value. They were not like the many seekers of buried treasure who plundered Ozark caves in the 1930s and 1950s, chasing legends and figments of the imagination.

11

Buried Treasure

11

**In the morning we lit our pitch-pine torches and started in. . . .
Nearly five hundred feet from the entrance we entered a big
arched room, the walls of which shone like polished silver. . . .
We thought we had found our eternal fortunes.**
—S. SCHOFFELMAYER, "Radium Mine in the Ozarks?"
Technical World Magazine, January 1913

In a region like the Ozarks, where folklore and legend cling to the
hills and people as tightly as cockleburs on pants legs, one would
expect to find a wealth of buried-treasure yarns. And so it is.

But to complicate matters, this supposed treasure is not just
buried beneath the floor of an old cabin or six paces from the
largest oak tree. Instead, legend invariably has it hidden in some
supposedly unexplored Ozark cave. When the details of the story are
revealed, it is a cave that was sealed by frightened Spaniards fleeing
hostile Indians or by Indians fleeing from Spaniards. Of course, one
of the survivors left behind a map that has survived to guide hope-
ful treasure hunters ever since.

Never mind that in all the years since the Spanish conquistadors
and French explorers and miners left the Missouri territories, not
one scrap of such buried treasure has been found by the innumer-
able treasure hunters who have spent fortunes and sometimes most
of their lives searching for it. Never mind that archaeologists have
spent a century digging up Indian artifacts and burials in caves and
have not once found legendary buried treasure.

Never mind that cavers have located, recorded, and explored

11

more than 6,200 caves in the state and mapped thousands of them in minute detail, and not one caver has discovered buried treasure. And never mind that for more than a century, geologists have been telling people that the bedrock of Missouri and the walls of Ozarks caves are not riddled with veins of gold, silver, or uranium ore.

Perhaps buried-treasure hunting is like antique collecting—it is the thrill of the hunt itself that motivates the seeker. Although buried treasure has been sought in Missouri caves since the middle of the nineteenth century, the two periods of history that witnessed the greatest explosion of this kind of activity in Ozark caves were the 1930s and the 1950s.

"Despite the negative pronouncements of men of science that no gold mines ever were found in the Ozark hills, the search for buried treasure goes on. It even grows in importance among certain natives and miners who occupy a greater portion of their time burrowing in the hills," according to an article in the *Kansas City Journal-Post* on September 6, 1931. The article also said that the men were hunting buried treasure because the area was economically depressed, and it was hard for them to find work at a living wage. "These treasure seekers not only work for nothing, but many of them have been known to borrow money on their homes to furnish a 'grub stake' so they can follow their leader, in every instance some smart native, who likewise is gambling for high stakes."

According to the news story, a cave beneath Breadtray Mountain, fifteen miles south of Reed's Spring in Stone County, that was scheduled to be flooded by the reservoir behind Table Rock Dam (then under construction), was said to have walls "covered with a solid mass of pure silver." Though the chances of finding such treasure are very slim, we may never know if the cave contains gold and silver because today it is inundated by Table Rock Lake.

When Bagnell Dam was being constructed to create the Lake of the Ozarks, Jim French, who lived in the Shawnee Bend area along the Osage River, did not like the idea of the coming Lake inundating a cave he thought contained buried treasure. On March 20, 1930, the *Miller County Autogram* reported that French claimed to have knowledge of treasure: "there has recently appeared at his home two strangers whom he believes to be of Indian blood, with maps and records of ancient trails hereabouts. French . . . says these men have plans to uncover a buried treasure. He believes it is located in Williams Cave, known locally as the Treasure Cave."

French owned a homestead just above the water level of the newly outlined Osage Lake (later named Lake of the Ozarks), and he bemoaned the fact that filling the lake would cover many springs and ancient tree markings, which he thought might be the key to Civil War loot and Spanish gold that he believed was hidden in local caves. French himself had spent a great deal of time looking for buried treasure.

Williams Cave, one of the better known caves inundated by the Lake of the Ozarks is close to the junction of the Osage and Grand Glaize rivers at the lake's nineteen-mile mark. Prior to inundation it was reported to be one of the most extensive caves in the Osage River valley. Its entrance is now beneath fifty feet of water.

These examples just happen to be of caves lost to inundation by two of Missouri's largest man-made lakes. Air-filled caves still accessible, which supposedly contain gold, silver, or other precious substances, are legion in the Ozarks. Believers, of course, always keep the location of their treasure cave a closely guarded secret. These secret caves also usually have "secret rooms."

Take for example the story of the lost Taylor silver mine cave in Ozark County. It was supposedly "rediscovered" in the 1950s. "One hundred pounds of . . . rock near Bakersfield, known to contain radio active minerals and possibly silver, are on their way to Rolla . . . for an official analysis," reported the West Plains newspaper. The newly discovered secret cave was thought to be the legendary lost Taylor silver mine where ore was supposedly "mined to make silver dollars shortly after the Civil War." The paper also reported that the cave explorers had found a secret room inside the cave that they had not yet explored.

According to another legend, "seven pony loads of dish gold" were let down into Ramsay Cave in Miller County during the Civil War. "However, earnest and expensive effort in 1929 certainly demonstrated that the treasure seekers dug in the wrong place if, indeed, there is a right place," said J Harlen Bretz in *Caves of Missouri*.

The entrance passage to Old Spanish Cave, near Reed's Spring in Stone County, ca. 1950. It is the only Missouri show cave discovered during the hunt for buried treasure. (Postcard; from the author's collection)

Gourd Creek Cave in Phelps County was supposedly explored by government officials in search of one hundred thousand dollars' worth of gold cached there by an Indian woman. Rumors circulate, as well, that young "geologists" from the university at Rolla have explored Gourd Creek Cave looking for buried gold, but when one pauses to analyze these rumors, problems emerge: Can these really be geologists? Geologists have maintained that Missouri geology does not favor the formation of gold and silver ore. The kind of gold treasure hunters seek has never been found, not even a trace of it, but the legend continues to grow.

At least one former show cave in Missouri was named Old Spanish Cave because it was discovered in the hunt for buried treasure. The treasure legend associated with this cave was once very popular in southwestern Missouri and produced a lot of newspaper copy. If names mean anything, there are three caves in Missouri named Treasure Cave, one each in the counties of Camden, Greene, and Shannon. There is a Money Cave in Dent County and Stone County, a Klondike Cave in Camden County, an Old Spanish Cave in Stone County, and a Spanish Treasure Cave in Carter County. But the word that shows up the most often in the hunt for hidden treasure is *silver*. There are caves with this word as part of their names—such as Sugar Silver Cave, Silver Cave, Silver Mine Cave, and Lost Silver Cave—in eight counties, all of them deep in the Missouri Ozark region.

Missouri caves have also been the focus of prospecting and mining for mineral resources such as lead, iron ore, barite, copper, and uranium. It was the hunt for uranium ore in the 1950s that produced the most ridiculous, destructive, and costly efforts to "strike it rich" in Missouri's caves. This farce took place in Butler Hollow and its tributaries in Barry County, on land that is now within the Mark Twain National Forest, about ten miles south of Cassville and not far from the Arkansas line.

Butler Hollow is noted for its caves and springs—Radium Spring and Carter Cave in particular. The caves are developed in limestone that rests upon the Chattanooga Shale. The shale produces enough natural radiation to make a scintillometer (an instrument that measures radiation) react as if the shale is uranium ore. The spring and caves first came to the attention of treasure hunters in 1913 when a very colorful account of the discovery of a cave in the hollow said to contain radium ore appeared in *Technical World Magazine*. Upon reading the account, treasure hunters, some of very questionable ethics and intentions, began a series of costly and destructive explorations in search of the elusive ore.

Between 1913 and 1958, the adventures of these "hard-rock miners" generated reams of newspaper copy. Prospecting, blasting, and digging went on for years. Some of the promoters were true scam artists; in one incident, they are believed to have salted one of the caves with carnotite ore from a uranium mine in Colorado. It got to the point where reputable geologists would not go near the valley for fear their very presence on the land would ruin their reputations. "Radium Cave is a notorious rat-hole for shady investments," said one geologist.

The physical damage done to the caves of the valley was considerable and enduring. The evidence is still lying about underground. In a visit to Carter Cave in 2006, one caver said, "We were surprised to see large quantities of mining relicts including wooden shoring, remains of wooden platforms, a wheelbarrow, old batteries, oil cans, a pump, lots of blasting cord and shot holes."

There is a downside to the hunt for buried treasure in caves—it inevitably involves blasting and digging that causes extensive damage to the resource for no reason better than a flight of fancy, which is inexcusable. Such activity destroys any archaeological resources that might be in the affected area, it damages the layers of sediments that enable geologists to unravel the geologic history of the cave, it damages or destroys any fossil remains that might be present, it disrupts the biological environment and has a harmful impact on fragile cave life, and it leaves the underground landscape unsightly and disfigured.

We can always hope that sooner or later buried-treasure hunters will learn from the failures of their predecessors, but considering human nature, that is probably asking too much. Today's technology is giving us some very sophisticated instruments for locating the invisible. Couple that with temptation, throw in a dash of misguided ambition, dig into deep pockets, burn the midnight oil boning up

on buried-treasure legends, and listen to the much-ballyhooed success of those who pursue the treasures that have actually been found
in ships that sank at sea hundreds of years ago, and you have the
recipe for trashing an Ozark cave.

During the late nineteenth century, people didn't even need the
lure of buried-treasure legends to help them trash a cave. All anyone
had to do was sponsor a "cave party."

12

Picnics and Parties

Are you going to the grand picnic at Green's Cave, July 3 & 4?
Two big days, plenty to eat, plenty to drink, all kinds of amuse-
ments . . . fireworks at 9:30 p.m. Large dancing floor, good
music, your friends expect to meet you there. Don't disappoint
them.
—Ad in *Sullivan Sentinel,* June 26, 1908

In 1895, D. N. Gideon made sure that the handbills advertising the
cave picnic at Saltpeter Cave were nailed up in all the towns
within a few hours' buggy ride from the cave. And just to make sure
the crowd would be large enough to guarantee that he and his partner, Joseph Schmuke, would clear a substantial profit, he informed
A. Hilton, the passenger traffic manager of the Frisco Railroad,
about the cave picnic. Hilton was always eager to promote events
along the Frisco line that would fill the passenger seats in his trains
between St. Louis and Springfield.

Gideon was a grocer and owned a general store in Stanton, a village along the railroad tracks in Franklin County. His partner,
Joseph Schmuke, was the Stanton hotelkeeper and also the operator
of one of Stanton's saloons. The event was planned for Saturday,
May 18, 1895. For Gideon and Schmuke, it was their first attempt at
staging a cave picnic. "This most wonderful Cave is situated two and
one-fourth miles southeast of Stanton, Mo. It is 750 x 130 ft. in
extent, and 70 ft. high, and in itself is worth a trip to see as a Grand
Work of Nature!" their handbill declared.

A 1895 poster announcing a picnic at Saltpeter Cave, now Meramec Caverns in Franklin County. (From *Meramec Caverns: Legendary Hideout of Jesse James,* by H. Dwight Weaver and Paul A. Johnson, 1977)

It has been fitted up into a Great Hall and Ball Room. In addition to the Great Hall are lesser halls and galleries, and a copious Saltpeter Spring supplies cool, refreshing and wholesome drink in abundance!

Two good Dancing floors have been fitted up, one in the large hall and the other in the shade of forest trees.

Music will be supplied by two of the best Bands in the county, and the best of Refreshments served in abundance.

The beautiful Meramec river flows past the Cave and affords the best swimming, boating, etc. A second cave is close by, with beautiful and wonderful scenes . . . torches will be furnished for its exploration.

The crowd that attended this first event at Saltpeter Cave found that the cave had a spacious entrance passage, and three hundred feet inside, it opened into an immense, circular chamber that had a hard-packed, smooth clay floor. There were even two wings to the ballroom that were also large chambers. The temperature of the cave was a pleasant sixty degrees, and there was almost no dripping water. Most of the entrance corridor and ballroom was pleasantly dry.

Besides the dance floors Gideon and Schmuke had constructed, they had secured lanterns about the walls and along the entrance corridor, built a bar in the cave, a platform for the musicians, cleared brush from the area outside the cave, tidied up the riverfront, and put the old wagon road down to the cave in passable shape.

The event was so successful that Gideon and Schmuke planned additional weekend parties. Word spread quickly up and down the Frisco line, and people from both St. Louis and Springfield began to attend the events. Hardly a summer weekend passed without some type of sponsored activity at the cave. Gideon and Schmuke prospered so well that they continued to sponsor summer dances and picnics at Saltpeter Cave until 1910.

Saltpeter Cave, known today as Meramec Caverns, was not the only cave where cave parties were held. Green's Cave and Fisher Cave, upstream from Saltpeter Cave, were also party sites. The Sullivan family of Sullivan, and the Schwarzer and Bienke families of Washington, Missouri, sponsored activities at Fisher Cave. "Cave parties are numerous these days," the *Sullivan Sentinel* reported in July 1901.

Occasionally the crowds were so large special arrangements were necessary. An event at Green's Cave in July 1903 was typical. Sixty people from St. Louis were involved. In October 1905 an even larger event was staged at Fisher Cave and entertained so many people the local paper declined to list them all by name but reported that, at the height of the party, "people attending came from Gray Summit, St. Louis, Kansas City and Pacific. . . . The party lasted for three or four days and employed three colored cooks."

The Franz Schwarzer family of Washington organized a "cave explorers club" to engage in spelunking and partying at numerous caves along the Meramec. S. H. Sullivan Jr. of Sullivan also organized a caving club. They were the first organized caving clubs in Missouri but were certainly not like the caving clubs we have today.

From 1885 to 1925, caves throughout the Ozarks witnessed the new phenomenon—a craze for cave picnics and parties. Electricity had arrived in the cities, but most homes and businesses did not yet have air-conditioning. Caves were an ideal setting for cool summertime fun.

In the late nineteenth and early twentieth centuries, the United States had an expanding middle class in urban centers that demanded leisure pursuits and were willing to pay for them. People turned to the outdoors for all kinds of recreational activities because it was also the age of America's first fitness and health craze. Mineral waters and health spas were all the rage. Swimming, boating, bicycling, roller-skating, and ice-skating were new fads. Resorts began to appear all across the Ozarks. The Chautauqua had come to life in the 1870s, and by the 1880s it was spreading from coast to coast in the United States. Caves were ideal settings for these extravagances of oratory, music, and other performance entertainment.

At Uhrig's Brewery Cave in St. Louis, the underground chambers were converted into a first-class theater by the St. Louis Coliseum Company, which had leased the property and constructed a new building over the cave entrance. When the underground venue, called the Coliseum, opened in 1909, the first user was the famed revivalist Gypsy Smith. In succeeding years Enrico Caruso sang there, Billy Sunday preached there, and Woodrow Wilson was nominated for president at the 1916 Democratic National Convention, said to have been held in the Coliseum.

Near Ash Grove in Greene County, a dance floor was constructed in a spacious chamber in Ash Grove Cave called the Ballroom. Spears Cave in Morgan County became the site of an annual Fourth of July picnic that drew crowds from several counties. The cave was often lighted so that people attending the event could explore the entire cave. "Splendid arrangements are being made for the celebration of the 4th at Spears Cave six miles southwest of Versailles," said the *Versailles Leader,* June 25, 1891. "The Versailles Gun Club will have a pigeon shoot, a premium of $5 being offered for the best score. Premiums will also be paid for the winners in sack racing and pole climbing. There will be an abundance of amusements."

At Stark Caverns, south of Eldon in Miller County, an underground dance floor and roller rink was built about two hundred feet back inside the cave. The parties there drew good crowds. In the winter, the cave stream would freeze inside the cave entrance, and ice-skating became an added entertainment. Dance pavilions existed in Crystal Cave at Joplin, St. James Tunnel Cave in Phelps County, Steckle Cave in Pulaski County, Harrington Cave in Perry County, Speakeasy Cave in Greene County, and at many other caves throughout the Ozarks.

The 1890–1920 period was a lively phase in Missouri cave history but also one of the most destructive. Onyx mining was in full bloom, and onyx novelties were everywhere in urban and resort gift shops. Unrestricted and unguided cave exploration was nearly always an added entertainment at cave picnics and parties if the cave was extensive or there were adjacent caves with easy access. Some of the caving led to major discoveries, but since no code of caving ethics had yet been established and destructive activities were not frowned upon during this period, the caves saw considerable damage. It became popular to take home "a piece of the cave" as a souvenir. Chunks of cave onyx were popular as doorstops. Stalactites wound up as mantelpieces and conversation starters, as inclusions in rock gardens, retaining walls, cottage walls, and whatever other ornamental use the owner of the souvenir fancied. Stalagmites even found their way into cemeteries as tombstones.

Luella Owen, who was doing research for her book *Cave Regions of the Ozarks and Black Hills of South Dakota,* published in 1898, noticed the destruction and spoke out against it:

> Unfortunately, most of the caves in this region [the Ozarks] have been deprived of great quantities of their beautiful adornment by visitors who are allowed to choose the best and remove it in such quantities as may suit their convenience and pleasure. Those who own the caves, and those who visit them, would do well to remember that if all the natural adornment should be allowed to remain in its original position, it would continue to afford pleasure to many persons for an indefinite time; but if broken, removed, and scattered the pleasure to a few will be comparatively little and that short-lived. The gift of beauty should always be honored and protected for the public good.

Unfortunately, hers was a voice crying out in the wilderness. Her book saw little public exposure and even when it was read during those years, it probably made little impression upon a generation for whom the word *inexhaustible* was applied to any underground resource, onyx cave formations in particular.

Cave owners allowed far too many of the picnic and party attendees to vandalize their caves. Far too many of the people who participated in the caving activities indulged in vandalism, breaking formations and defacing cave walls, ceilings, and boulders with carved, smoked, and painted names, dates, and other graffiti. The damage that was done to cave formations endures to this day. Much of the disfigurement that we see in both wild caves and show caves dates to this period. Most of the damaged formations will be disfigured forever. Nature cannot heal them, even in the lifetimes of hundreds of generations of people.

Modern technology has given us the tools to repair some of the damage to cave formations, but only if the broken pieces are not too shattered and are still lying nearby in the cave. Cavers are repairing some of the broken stalactites, stalagmites, and columns in Missouri caves, but it is painstaking, time-consuming work, most of which will probably never be seen nor appreciated except by fellow cavers. It is admirable work done out of love for the cave, but so much damage was done to Ozark caves during that one period that repairing one formation is like polishing one seashell on a shell-littered beach the size of an ocean.

Unfortunately, our caves are still under attack by vandals. The tradition of writing names and dates in caves continues to this day in wild caves, as does the indiscriminate handling, breaking, and destruction of cave formations.

It happened as recently as five years ago at River Bluff Cave at Springfield, Missouri. According to Matt Forir, lead paleontologist at River Bluff Cave, three young men broke into the gated cave, carved their initials at the base of a beautiful cave formation, and then wrote that they explored the cave (illegally) on April 26, 2002. They also scattered the fossil bones of a snake and left footprints in sensitive areas noted for fossil animal tracks. Fortunately, the vandals were caught, convicted, and sentenced to three years in prison. "I am somewhat sure that this has been the worst punishment for cave vandalism in the state and probably the country," said Forir. Fortunately, some of the damage was repairable to the extent that it is not apparent to a casual observer, but this kind of resource destruction always leaves scars that can never be healed.

At the beginning of the twentieth century, there were at least a few responsible promoters of cave picnics and parties. When Gideon and Schmuke held events in Saltpeter Cave, people were not allowed to litter the cave or write on the walls. During one of the caving expeditions in 1901, a major discovery was made in Saltpeter Cave—unbelievably beautiful upper levels of the cave were found. Until then, the cave had been thought to end just beyond the ballroom. Immediately afterward, that portion of the cave became a new attraction, and people who came to the dances were allowed to tour the upper sections—but they were not allowed to handle or break formations and not permitted to disfigure the cave with graffiti. As a consequence, in 1933, Lester B. Dill was able to open the cave to the public as a show cave, and since that date millions of people have had their breath taken away by the exquisite beauty of the Stage Curtains in Meramec Caverns.

Show caves, which made their first appearance in the 1880s, have definitely made a difference in Missouri.

13

Show Caves

The Ozarks would give up almost everything before she would her caves and rivers, they mean too much as tourist attractions.
—JOE TAYLOR, "Tourist Gold the Buried Treasure,"
Missouri Magazine, June 1934

Caves were among the first natural geographic features of Missouri to be commercially developed and promoted as tourist attractions. About 10 percent of the people who come to the state each year as tourists visit a show cave. Missouri has more show caves than any other state, and the caves are widely known for their beauty and history.

A *show cave* is defined in Missouri law as "any cave or cavern wherein trails have been created and some type of lighting provided by the owner or operator for purpose of exhibition to the general public as a profit or nonprofit enterprise, wherein a fee is generally collected for entry." The number of show caves open to the public in Missouri has varied from year to year and decade to decade, depending upon the circumstances that attend each cave operation, regardless of whether the ownership is federal, state, or private. Over the past 150 years, more than fifty Missouri caves have been exhibited to the public as show caves.

A *commercial cave* is any cave or cavern that is developed and operated for profit, be it for exhibition, as a theater, as a restaurant, or for some other commercial activity. A commercial show cave, therefore, is a commercial cave that is open to the public primarily to exhibit its natural features.

A *wild cave* is any cave in its natural condition—a cave that has not been modified for some human purpose. These are the caves most closely identified with the activities of organized spelunking groups who explore, map, and study caves. Some generally noncaving segments of the public, however, do occasionally go caving in wild caves through structured outdoor educational and recreational adventure programs. Both the Missouri Department of Natural Resources and the Missouri Department of Conservation have and use wild caves that they own and manage for educating the public about cave resources.

Tumbling Creek Cave (Ozark Underground Laboratory) in Taney County has visitor trails, yet it fits none of the above categories. Its visitors are generally limited to college students during science course work, or geologists, biologists, and other scientists doing cave-related research.

Notable commercial caves of the early and mid-1800s included a host of caves in St. Louis that were converted into storage and cooling facilities for breweries and wineries, underground beer gardens, theaters, mushroom farms, and cheese-manufacturing plants. English Cave, which is believed to still exist beneath Benton Park in south St. Louis, and Uhrig's Cave, a former brewery cave along Market Street, were actually operated as show caves for brief periods between the 1840s and the 1890s.

Most of the old St. Louis Brewery caves are now sealed and no longer accessible, and some have actually been filled in or otherwise destroyed. One of the former brewery caves in St. Louis that still exists in fragments is Cherokee Cave, which became a celebrated Missouri show cave from 1945 to 1961. The cave lies underground between Interstate Highway 55, Demenil Place, and Cherokee Street. Construction along I-55 in the 1960s partially destroyed the cave, which was famous for its Lemp Brewery history and its rich, fossil-embedded sediments that contain ice-age animal remains.

Show cave development in the United States began with Mammoth Cave in Kentucky, which was first operated as a show cave in 1816. For the next 140 years, it became the model after which many privately owned show cave attractions were modeled. Even the given names of the features in Mammoth Cave have been widely copied by subsequent show cave developers.

Samuel Clemens, better known as Mark Twain, could easily be called the patron saint of the Missouri show cave industry. His book *The Adventures of Tom Sawyer* brought fame to Hannibal and the limestone cave just south of the city then known as McDowell's Cave. In his book, Mark Twain calls it McDougal's Cave, and the book's success led to the cave's commercial development. Mark Twain Cave was opened to the public in 1886 and, by contemporary definitions, became Missouri's first official show cave.

MISSOURI SHOW CAVES

NAME	NEAREST TOWN	COUNTY	DATE
Opened before 1900			
Mark Twain Cave	Hannibal	Marion	1886
Crystal Cave	Springfield	Greene	1893
Marvel Cave	Branson	Stone	1894
Sequiota Cave	Springfield	Greene	1896
Onondaga Cave*	Leasburg	Crawford	1897
Doling Park Cave	Springfield	Greene	1898
Opened from 1900 to 1929			
Ancient Grotto	Eldon	Miller	1900
Cleveland Cave	Monegaw Springs	St. Clair	1900
Crystal Cave	Joplin	Jasper	1908
Ozark Wonder Cave	Noel	McDonald	1916
Fantastic Caverns	Springfield	Greene	1920
Talking Rocks Cave	Kimberling City	Stone	1921
Old Spanish Cave	Reeds Spring	Stone	1924
Bluff Dwellers Cave	Noel	McDonald	1925
Smittle Cave	Grovespring	Wright	1925
Mt. Shira Cave	Noel	McDonald	1926
Fisher Cave*	Sullivan	Franklin	1928
Mushroom Cave	Sullivan	Franklin	1929

Opened from 1930 to 1949

*Cathedral Caverns**	Leasburg	Crawford	1930
Lewis Cave	Wilderness	Ripley	1930
Stalactite Cave	West Plains	Howell	1930
Crystal Caverns	Cassville	Barry	1930
Keener Cave	Williamsville	Wayne	1930
*Round Spring Caverns**	Round Spring	Shannon	1932
Jacobs Cave	Versailles	Morgan	1932
Meramec Caverns	Stanton	Franklin	1933
Flanders Cave	Bagnell	Miller	1933
Wonder Cave	Reed's Spring	Stone	1935
Big Niangua Cave	Camdenton	Camden	1938
Truitt's Cave	Lanagan	McDonald	1938
Cave Spring Onyx Caverns	Van Buren	Carter	1940
Cardareva Cave	Ellington	Shannon	1940
Mystery Cave	Noel	McDonald	1945
Cherokee Cave	City of St. Louis		1945
Cameron Cave	Hannibal	Marion	1947
Bridal Cave	Camdenton	Camden	1948
Mystic River Cave*	Camdenton	Camden	1948

Opened from 1950 to 1990

Stark Caverns	Eldon	Miller	1950
Great Spirit Cave*	Waynesville	Pulaski	1952
*Ozark Caverns**	Linn Creek	Camden	1952
Wind Cave	Noel	McDonald	1953
Indian Cave	Waynesville	Pulaski	1953
Indian Burial Cave	Osage Beach	Miller	1960
Honey Branch Cave	Ava	Douglas	1961
Civil War Cave	Ozark	Christian	1962
Boone Cave*	Rocheport	Boone	1964
*Devil's Well**	Gladden	Shannon	1965
Rebel Cave	Piedmont	Wayne	1965
Arrow Point Cave	Brumley	Miller	1967
Emerald Grotto	Round Spring	Shannon	1969

Emerald Lake Cave	Greenfield	Dade	1972
Neongwah Bear Cave	Camdenton	Camden	1982
Onyx Mountain Caverns*	St. Robert	Pulaski	1990

* An asterisk indicates the cave is currently operated by a state or federal agency. *Italic type* means the cave is believed or is known to be still in commercial operation. All dates should be considered approximate.

Between 1900 and 1929, twelve privately owned wild caves were developed and opened to the public.

Ancient Grotto, Cleveland Cave, Crystal Cave, Mt. Shira Cave, and Mushroom Cave were open to the public for only a short period of time. Fantastic Caverns was first operated as Temple Caverns. Talking Rocks Cavern began as Fairy Cave.

McDonald County saw an unusual wave of show cave development from 1915 to 1940 when J. A. "Dad" Truitt, known in his day as the "Caveman of the Ozarks," was instrumental in opening a number of show caves in that county. In fact, the 1920s, 1930s, and 1940s were important decades for show cave development all over America largely due to Truitt's success in southwestern Missouri, the opening of Carlsbad Caverns in New Mexico, the unusual circumstances of the death of Floyd Collins, who was hopelessly trapped in a Kentucky sand cave in 1925, and the international fame of Russell T. Neville. Neville was a pioneer cave photographer who shed light upon the beauty of caves to appreciative audiences throughout the world through public presentations of his work.

The stock market crash in October 1929 ushered in the Great Depression. One might think that, during the Depression years of the 1930s and the World War II years of the 1940s, very few caves would have been developed, but such was not the case. Between 1930 and 1949, Missouri saw the opening of at least eighteen new show caves.

Part of this surge was brought about by uncertainty about the future. The economic collapse was nationwide, but the privations of the Depression were not as severe in the Ozarks as they were in major metropolitan areas. Some people, however, saw turning a wild cave on their property into a show cave as a way of earning extra income and providing some additional financial security. Many of these developments were poorly planned, poorly financed, and involved caves that had very little to recommend them to the public as show caves. They were also opened before the state of Missouri established safety standards for show cave operations.

It should be noted that several of the show cave operations during this period were associated with resorts that offered additional attractions to the public, such as rental cabins and swimming, fishing, hunting, and other recreational opportunities. Under such circumstances, it was primarily the people who stayed at the resorts that visited the caves.

Cathedral Cave in Crawford County was originally opened as Missouri Caverns. Bunch Cave in Camden County was operated commercially for two seasons as Big Niangua Cave. Mystic River Cave at Ha Ha Tonka State Park is still open to visitors during a few weeks of the year but only as a wild cave adventure. Most of the year it is closed to protect an endangered bat colony.

The period 1950 to 1990 was the last great phase of show cave development in Missouri and gave the state fifteen new show caves, most of which are no longer open to the public.

Stark Caverns is currently known as Fantasy World Caverns. Great Spirit Cave was opened to the public as Inca Cave. Indian Burial Cave was originally known as Big Mouth Cave. Ozark Caverns was opened to the public as Coakley Cave. Civil War Cave was originally called Smallin Cave and since being closed has regained its original name. Boone Cave has regained its original name of Rocheport Cave. Arrow Point Cave was originally known as Wright Cave. Emerald Grotto is better known as The Sinks. Emerald Lake Cave was originally called Martin Cave. Neongwah Bear Cave is generally referred to simply as Bear Cave. Onyx Mountain Caverns was originally Onyx Cave or Boiling Springs Cave.

With so many show caves being opened to the public, Missouri legislation was enacted in the 1950s charging the Missouri Division of Labor Standards with responsibility for giving each show cave an annual safety inspection. This inspection is designed to ensure that the cave is structurally sound and that all trails and man-made struc-

The famed Lily Pad Room in an upper level of Onondaga Cave, in Onondaga Cave State Park near Leasburg in Crawford County. The decorative chamber features cave formations that have formed both above and below water. (Photo by James Vandike)

tures within the cave are safe for public use. Missouri show caves have an excellent safety record.

Until the 1960s, no government agency operated a show cave in Missouri. The creation of the Ozark National Scenic Riverways along the Current River transferred ownership of Round Spring Caverns, previously a privately owned show cave, to the National Park Service.

In the 1960s, the Missouri show cave industry also established its own trade organization, the Missouri Caves Association, which went a long way toward replacing fierce competition with friendly and beneficial cooperation. Early in Missouri show cave history, cave "advertising warfare" was not uncommon and even led to lawsuits when the show caves were close together or their visitors had to use the same state or county road to reach them. Today, the Missouri

An early view of the Ballroom in Fisher Cave in Meramec State Park, ca. 1928. The man on the right, wearing a hat, is believed to be the guide, Lester B. Dill, the developer and first operator of the show cave. In front of the group are the remains of the last dance floor built in the cave. Dances were held in the cave from about 1890 to 1920, sponsored by various local families. (Postcard; from the author's collection)

Cave Association is also allied with the show caves of Arkansas. Many of the show caves of both states are also members of the National Caves Association. There are more than two hundred show caves in the United States.

The Missouri Department of Natural Resources was established in 1974. Not long after, the department's Division of State Parks acquired a number of properties for parks and historic sites, and some of them contained cave resources. Several caves that had been privately operated show caves then became state operations. These caves included Onondaga Cave, Cathedral Cave, Mystic River Cave, and Ozark Caverns, although Mystic River Cave, located in Ha Ha Tonka State Park in Camden County, was not continued as a show cave operation.

The first seventy years of the twentieth century was the golden age for Missouri show caves. Of the fifteen caves that have been developed since 1950, only three are still available to the public—Ozark Caverns, Devil's Well, and Neongwah Bear Cave.

Devil's Well in Shannon County is an oddity because the cave is not actually toured. Visitors simply stand on a viewing platform in the sinkhole entrance, where it is possible to see the gigantic, electrically lighted underground lake room a hundred feet below. Neongwah Bear Cave is a small secondary attraction in Camden County located along a nature trail in Thunder Mountain Park, which is owned by Bridal Cave near Camdenton. Bear Cave is available primarily to school groups and other organizations who are taken on nature walks along the trail.

Many factors have contributed to the conclusion of Missouri's golden age of show cave development. The reasons are complex and numerous but include the construction of interstate and limited-access highways coupled with outdoor advertising restrictions and billboard regulations that went into effect in the 1970s. Billboards have generally become too expensive for most show cave operations to finance easily. Cave billboards currently in use are primarily those that existed before sign regulations came into effect and were grandfathered in when sign laws were passed.

In Missouri, show cave operators can now purchase several "directional signs" from the Missouri Highway Department. These small signs are erected on the state right-of-way near the cave's turnoff by the highway department itself. They are important to a show cave operation because they give last-minute directional information for anyone already looking for a particular show cave. But it takes an interesting and compelling commercial billboard to inspire a traveler to pull off the highway and visit a show cave.

Most show caves cannot afford the daily newspaper, radio, or TV advertising necessary to be an effective medium for attracting substantial numbers of visitors to a remote cave location. Show cave operations have wasted millions of dollars over the years trying to find ways to advertise effectively using these media. In the end, it invariably comes down to having a good highway location, outdoor advertising, widely distributed and attractive brochures, and word-of-mouth publicity. If a visitor has been to the cave before and had an enjoyable and worthwhile experience, it is likely he or she will

Massive canopy and drapery formations decorate the halls of Cathedral Cave in Onondaga Cave State Park. First shown to the public in 1930, the cave was discovered by Lester B. Dill in the 1920s. (Photo by James Vandike)

return and also influence others to visit the same attraction. The problem for the show cave is surviving long enough as a commercial venture to build a following of devoted fans. Federal- and state-owned show caves are subsidized by tax dollars; privately owned show caves are not.

The travel habits of the American public have also changed. Most travelers are not willing to leave the highways and drive several miles or more into a rural area to visit a single cave attraction that probably will not occupy them for more than an hour. They seek major recreational destination areas, and most show caves are not located in such areas where there is a captive audience. Grandeur, size, and historic value no longer guarantee a developer that his or her show cave will be a successful, long-lived commercial operation. Show

Originally called Maxey Cave, this cave was renamed Inca Cave when it was commercialized in 1950. The cave was shown to the public for about fifteen years. Today it is called Great Spirit Cave and is owned by the Missouri Department of Conservation; it is now a gated sanctuary for endangered bats. (Photo by Gerald Massie, Missouri State Archives)

caves are far more expensive to develop, promote, operate, and maintain today than ever before in Missouri show cave history.

It is interesting to note that of the six caves opened to the public before the year 1900, four of them are still in operation a century later, a success ratio considerably higher than for the other development periods.

Show caves have long been a major part of the backbone of Missouri tourism. Between 1900 and 1970, tens of millions of people visited Missouri show caves. At the height of show cave popularity in the 1950s and 1960s, summer travelers could depend upon finding more than two dozen show caves to visit in Missouri in any given year. Today, that number is considerably diminished, but more than half a million people still tour Missouri show caves each year, and as any fan of show caves will tell you, the Missouri landscape is just as beautiful beneath the surface as it is above.

For the privilege of getting to see these remarkable show caves of Missouri, we owe tribute to Missouri's pioneer show cave men and women.

14

Cave Men and Cave Women

The beauty of Missouri is more than skin deep. . . . The state is
as beautiful below the ground as it is above.
—MISSOURI TOURISM COMMISSION BOOKLET, 1972

In 1966, the *Franklin County Tribune* ran bold headlines that
announced "America's Number One Caveman Is a Franklin
County Resident." The article featured Lester B. Dill, the owner of
Meramec Caverns.

Dill grew up on a farm along the Meramec River on land that
today is part of Meramec State Park. Many of the caves in the valley
have large openings and spacious underground chambers where
local people sponsored lavish cave parties during the summer
months in the early 1900s. Cave exploring was nearly always a part
of such social events. Dill and his brothers made pocket change by
making themselves available as local caving guides.

Following the dedication of Meramec State Park in 1928, Dill's
father, Thomas Benton Dill, became the first park superintendent.
By this time Les Dill was thirty years old. The Dills were able to con-
vince the state to open Fisher Cave to the public as a special attraction in the park, and Les Dill operated the cave as a concessionaire.
But in the early 1930s, when state politics changed, Thomas Benton
Dill lost his position as superintendent, and Les Dill lost the cave
concession. The younger man immediately launched a quest to
find a nearby wild cave outside the state park that he could com-
mercialize. He found just such a cave north of the park called
Saltpeter Cave.

On May 1, 1933, Dill opened Saltpeter Cave to the public as Meramec Caverns. With the help of family he was able to transform the attraction into one of the greatest show caves Missouri has ever known. It is still one of the most popular show caves in the nation.

Missouri tourism history is enriched by the colorful stories of the pioneer show cave men and women of the closing years of the nineteenth century and the early decades of the twentieth century. Examples include the Cameron family of Mark Twain Cave; the Lynch family of Marvel Cave; the Powell family of Fairy Cave; the Mann family of Crystal Cave; the Truitt family of McDonald County; the Bradford family of Onondaga Cave; and the Dill family of Meramec Caverns. And it all began with Mark Twain.

In the 1870s and 1880s, a sequence of events occurred at Hannibal, Missouri, that changed the life of Evan T. Cameron, the son of John Cameron. John Cameron owned a dairy farm at the mouth of Cave Hollow, just south of town. In the same hollow was McDowell's Cave, which had been used by Mark Twain as a setting for some of the adventures of his fictional character, Tom Sawyer, in *The Adventures of Tom Sawyer*, published in 1876.

The Fielder and Stilwell families of Hannibal owned the cave. In the early 1880s, so many people wanted to see it that John East was hired to take people through the cave. His fee of ten cents per person was shared with the cave's owners.

John Cameron's son, Evan T., decided it was also a good opportunity for him to earn extra money. With his father's blessing and the permission of the cave's owners, he hung his own "cave guide" shingle in front of the Cameron home along the road leading to the cave. He charged twenty-five cents for adults and ten cents for children. The year was 1886. By this time, people were calling the attraction Mark Twain Cave.

In 1923, Evan T. Cameron, then fifty-eight years old and the operator of the family dairy farm, bought the cave property. Between 1886 and 1923, he had managed the cave operation for its various owners. During that time he had established a permanent tour route through the cave's maze of passageways, built a small ticket building near the entrance, purchased lanterns that people could carry for

Truman Powell, newspaper publisher and writer, wrote late-nineteenth-century articles about Marble Cave (Marvel Cave) that were instrumental in the opening of the cave to the public in 1886. The Powell family later developed Fairy Cave, now called Talking Rocks Cavern. Both caves are in the Branson area of Stone County. (State Historical Society of Missouri, Columbia)

lighting, hired cave guides, and advertised the attraction as Mark Twain Cave. The cave was open on a daily basis year-round.

Evan T. Cameron died in 1944 and was succeeded by his son, Archie K. Cameron, who was born in 1897 and raised in Cave Hollow. Like his father, Archie became a devotee of the cave. Following a hitch in the army during World War I, he returned home, married, and assumed management of the cave. Archie was at the helm of the operation for thirty-one years; he died in 1976.

In the same year that Mark Twain Cave became Missouri's first show cave (1886), the Truman Powell family moved from Lamar, Missouri, to the Ozarks and settled in Stone County. Truman Powell, the father of six sons, was a newspaper publisher and established the Stone County *Oracle* at Galena. Marble Cave (Marvel Cave) was just sixteen miles away. The cave fascinated Powell, and he began writing newspaper stories about it. Historians believe it was through one of Powell's stories that William H. Lynch, a Canadian, heard about Marble Cave. He made a visit to the wilderness site and was so taken by the cave's mystique that he bought it.

On October 18, 1894, the Lynch family opened Marble Cave to the public. Visitors entered by climbing down a long ladder into the gigantic, domed Cathedral Room, where a platform was built and a piano installed. William Lynch's young daughters, Genevieve and Miriam, entertained visitors by playing the piano and singing opera tunes. The cave was so remote in those days that it had few visitors and proved unprofitable as a commercial venture. William Lynch, originally a dairyman by trade, closed the cave operation and returned to Canada, hoping to get back to the Ozarks when he had recouped his financial loses.

In his absence, Truman Powell's son, William, settled near Marble Cave and began showing it to the public without the consent or knowledge of William Lynch. The Lynch family was gone for more than a decade, and the Powells thought they could claim the property through squatter's rights, but when the Lynch family returned, William Lynch proved legal ownership and the Powells had to quit the property.

Not far from Marble Cave, on land adjacent to the homestead of Waldo Powell, was a cave of considerable beauty that the Powells had explored in 1896. It was small in comparison to Marble Cave, but they bought the cave property in 1907, named the new attraction Fairy Cave, and opened it to the public. Waldo Powell assumed management of the cave.

But Fairy Cave was not the sole domain of the men in the Powell family during their ownership. Miss Hazel Rowena Powell, a granddaughter of Truman Powell, also became a part of the Fairy Cave operation. Distinguished in her own right, her career included that of teacher, practical nurse, dressmaker, potter, lecturer, cave guide, and author. In 1953 she published *Adventures Underground in the Caves of Missouri*, a small guidebook to Missouri show caves. There were fourteen show caves in Missouri at that time, and her book was a milestone because it was the first book published that was devoted exclusively to Missouri caves. Fairy Cave was owned and operated by the Powell family until the 1970s, when it was purchased by the Herschend family of Silver Dollar City fame and was then renamed Talking Rocks Cavern.

After solving their dispute with the Powells over the ownership of

Marble Cave, the Lynch family was determined to reopen Marble Cave and give the show cave business a second try. The Lynch sisters went back to playing the piano and singing for guests in the cave's huge Cathedral Room. The stage built in the cave served many public events. William Lynch also built facilities on the property to house visitors and constructed a special road from Branson to the cave.

While their father busied himself with improving the property and attracting business, Genevieve and Miriam managed the cave, which is huge, deep, and extensive. The Lynch sisters became accomplished spelunkers and show cave operators. During their lifetime they were so devoted to the cave, its mysteries and its commercial operation, they had no time for suitors or marriage. But time found them. By 1950, their father had passed on and they were too old and frail to continue the work. By this time the name of the cave had been changed to Marvel Cave. They leased it to their good friends—Hugo and Mary Herschend and their sons Jack and Pete—who, as the years passed, carried the business to heights of greater success than William Henry Lynch would ever have dreamed possible. Thanks to the Herschends, Silver Dollar City, one of the nation's oldest and most popular theme parks, was born on the mountain peak above Marvel Cave.

There were other "spinsters" in the Ozarks, as single women were known in those days, who were accomplished cave women. These women, the three Mann sisters, were in the hills just north of Springfield at Crystal Cave in Greene County. They, too, followed in the footsteps of their ambitious father, Alfred Mann, in the late 1800s and became a legend in their own time.

Crystal Cave opens in a small sinkhole on a gently sloping hillside. The cave consists of a complex series of highly decorated chambers. It was originally known as Jenkins Cave. Alfred Mann, a cabinetmaker by trade, came to the United States from England in 1870. In 1887, he purchased the Jenkins Cave property after seeing the cave. By the spring of 1893, Alfred Mann had the cave grounds cleared, a road put in, and trails constructed in the cave. He opened it to the public in the summer of 1893 as Crystal Cave.

Agnes (Missy), Ada, and Margaret (Maggie), Alfred's daughters,

The Mann sisters, Agnes (Missy), Ada, and Margaret (Maggie), stand-
ing in front of the family home on the hill close to Crystal Cave, in
Greene County north of Springfield, ca. 1950. (Courtesy Estle
Funkhouser; from the author's collection)

were teenagers at this time. The oldest was eighteen, the youngest
fourteen. They were bright, well-disciplined, lively girls, raised by a
stern, demanding, religious father. As the years passed, the girls'
names became synonymous with Crystal Cave. People far and wide
wondered why the Mann sisters never married and why they clung
so steadfastly to the cave.

For the sisters, the problem was their father. Brilliant and edu-
cated though he was, he was also unyielding and domineering.
Advancing age made him even worse. The dedicated efficiency of
his daughters led him to the conviction that it was in the family's
best financial interests for his daughters to remain single and to continue managing the cave operation.

Only Missy, the oldest, made an effort to break away. For seven
years she was courted by an ambitious young man, but in the end,

"Dad" Truitt in Bluff Dweller's Cave, McDonald County, Noel, Missouri. (Postcard; from the author's collection)

he was driven away by Alfred Mann's manipulative behavior. While the sisters managed the cave, their father managed them.

Alfred Mann died in 1925, followed by his wife in 1930. The Mann sisters continued with the cave. Missy, the first to pass on, died in 1960. Ada and Margaret, aging, surrounded themselves with animal companions. They had so many cats and dogs living with them in the old family home on the hill that only rarely did anyone choose to visit them. The cave's business had declined, and if a visitor rang the bell by the cave to alert them at the house, the visitor would have to wait while one or the other of the two women hobbled down to the cave to guide the tour.

After the death of the Mann sisters, Estle Funkhouser, a retired Springfield schoolteacher, operated the cave for a number of years. Estle also had never married. She was an energetic lady and a delightful cave guide. She had known the Mann sisters quite well and had been their lifelong friend. Amazingly, the one suitor in Missy's youth had been none other than Estle Funkhouser's father!

Marvel, Fairy, and Crystal caves are in southwest Missouri. Except for the northeast quarter of the state, where Mark Twain Cave is located, southwest Missouri was the cradle of show cave development between 1886 and 1926, after which much of the interest in developing show caves moved north and east into the heartland of the Ozarks. The last individual in southwest Missouri to officially lay claim to the title of "cave man" was J. A. Truitt, affectionately known as "Dad" Truitt.

Truitt was born in 1865 to Levi and Jane Truitt of Shelbyville, Illinois. He became a man of many trades when he reached adulthood. Before he and his wife, Lenah LaFaun, settled in McDonald County in 1915, he had tried several occupations, including that of farmer, streetcar conductor in St. Louis during the 1904 World's Fair, salesman, and guide at Cave of the Winds in Colorado Springs, Colorado. When he and Lenah arrived at Elk Springs, Missouri, in 1914, they bought a resort along the Elk River and began making improvements.

Money was scarce. Dad Truitt worked at several jobs simultaneously in order to make ends meet while he struggled to revive the resort's business. He wore such hats as mayor, justice of the peace, law officer, and depot agent. His need for cash was so demanding that he even searched for buried treasure in what little leisure time he had during the summer months. One summer, he found an opening in a bluff on his property that was exhaling a strong current of chilly air, a sure sign that a cave lay inside the hill. Dollar signs and visions of throngs of people coming to his Elk Springs Resort flashed before his eyes.

Truitt proceeded to enlarge the opening and explore the cave. He opened it to the public as Ozark Cave (later called Ozark Wonder Cave) in 1916. It became the first show cave in McDonald County. It was small, but well decorated, and while it was in no way comparable to Cave of the Winds for grandeur, it was a bonanza for Dad Truitt.

He was in the "Land of a Million Smiles," where tourists and fishermen were abundant. Having no competition, his new show cave boomed with visitors. Dad Truitt had, in his own way, discovered the buried treasure he was looking for. Before long, newspapers as far as two hundred miles away were calling him the "Cave Man of the Ozarks."

Dad Truitt turned his attention to other nearby locations where caves were rumored to be and began looking for a new cave to develop. Over the next forty years he would make his living selling real estate and opening show caves for himself and others in McDonald County. Truitt tried to transform more than half a dozen wild caves of McDonald County into show caves. He would develop a cave, promote it to get it going, then sell it and move on to a new site. For him, each cave was a new adventure.

When, decades earlier, Truitt had worked as a St. Louis streetcar conductor during the St. Louis World's Fair, he may have learned about Onondaga Cave near Leasburg, Missouri, and it may have encouraged him to try the show cave business. Dad Truitt did not give up caves until he retired in the 1950s and moved to Sulphur Springs, Arkansas. He left behind a unique legacy in McDonald County, Missouri.

Farther northeast in the state in Crawford County another legacy was born in 1886 when Charlie Christopher discovered a cave while exploring a spring outlet near the Meramec River. He and his friend

John P. Eaton attempted to open the cave to the public in 1897, calling it the "Mammoth Cave of Missouri." Their venture was unsuccessful. They subsequently sold the cave to four St. Louis men, who established the Onondaga Mining Company. The company planned to mine the cave's enormous onyx deposits for use in buildings to be constructed for the 1904 St. Louis World's Fair.

The mining venture failed. To recoup financial losses, the company made the cave available to World's Fair visitors as a special attraction, calling it Onondaga Cave. Round-trip excursions to the cave were booked at the fair. Visitors made the eighty-mile one-way trip to Leasburg in Crawford County on the Frisco Railroad line. Once at Leasburg, a horse-drawn surrey called the Onondaga Cave Bus took them to the cave where they were given overnight lodging, good meals, and tours of the gigantic cave before their return trip to St. Louis.

After the World's Fair, the cave remained open to the general public for regular daily tours, and Philip A. Franck managed the operation until 1913, when the cave was leased to Robert (Bob) E. and Mary C. Bradford of St. Louis. The lease contained an option to buy, and the Bradfords soon bought the cave. For the next thirty years, they shared the workload and an unexpected burden this cave brought to their lives.

At first the Bradfords prospered at Onondaga Cave in its Meramec River valley setting, but adjacent to the Onondaga Cave property was land owned by the Indian Creek Land Company. Boundary disputes erupted between the company and the Bradfords when it was discovered that Onondaga Cave's commercial route ran beneath both properties. Costly lawsuits resulted, and the Bradfords lost in court, forcing them to cease using the portion of Onondaga that ran beneath Indian Creek Land Company property. It was a blow for the Bradfords, because that section of the cave was very desirable, consisting of a series of large chambers and passageways lavishly adorned with beautiful cave formations.

Matters only grew worse when Dr. William H. Mook, a renowned dermatologist associated with the Bernard Free Skin and Cancer Hospital of St. Louis, leased Indian Creek Land Company property over the cave and proceeded to open the section of Onondaga Cave

Lester B. Dill, 1898–1980. A legend in his own time, Dill was often billed as "America's Number One Caveman." (Photo by H. Dwight Weaver, 1976)

that ran beneath that property, calling it Missouri Caverns. Fences were put up inside the gigantic cave to separate the two properties and the show cave operations. But even underground, the boundary was disputed. Rock throwing and verbal battles often took place along the fences between cave guides working for the companies.

To make matters worse for the Bradfords, the public had to travel a single road to reach both show caves. The road passed by the Missouri Caverns entrance before it reached the Onondaga Cave entrance, giving Missouri Caverns an unfair advantage. As a consequence, a bitter "cave war" erupted along the county road. Both operations employed people to lure visitors from the other's attraction.

The cave war was not settled until after the deaths of both Bradford and Mook, when Charles Rice of St. Louis formed the Crawford County Caverns Association and leased both properties. After Rice died in 1949, the two caves were sold to Lester B. Dill and Lyman Riley at nearby Meramec Caverns. Lyman Riley assumed management of Onondaga Cave. The Missouri Caverns section was reunited with the Onondaga Cave tour route, and the entrance to Missouri Caverns was closed.

In the 1960s, a new threat to Onondaga Cave loomed on the horizon: the U.S. Army Corps of Engineers plan to dam the Meramec River for flood control and recreation. If built, the Meramec Dam reservoir would inundate much of Onondaga Cave as well as many other caves in the Meramec River valley.

A media and political battle was waged to defeat government plans to build the dam, and flames were fanned by sensational and often misleading news stories. Environmentalists, cave enthusiasts, sportsmen, conservationists, engineers, journalists, businessmen, citizens, and politicians all chose sides and locked horns. In the end, the plan to build the Meramec Dam was defeated by a vote of the people who had the most of lose if the dam were to be built—residents of the counties who would feel the greatest impact of the dam and reservoir, and landowners of the valley.

Lester B. Dill had become the sole owner of Onondaga Cave by this time. Because of the majestic nature of Onondaga Cave, the richness of its history, and his desire to see the cave placed in a position where it would never again be threatened by the schemes of men, he wanted to see the cave become a state park. Unfortunately, his death intervened in 1980. Dill's estate, the Nature Conservancy, and the Missouri legislature then worked together to preserve Onondaga Cave for future generations. Onondaga Cave State Park was dedicated in 1982.

The pioneer show cave men and women of Missouri were among the forerunners who heralded a new attitude among Missourians about the value and significance of the state's wonderful cave resources.

15

Changing Attitudes

The Missouri Ozarks has more than [its] share of caves and caverns, many of them unexplored. Though she may not have the largest caves in the world, Missouri makes up for lack of size with number and variety.
—A. C. BURRILL, Curator, Missouri State Museum
in *Circular No. 125,* 1925

The twentieth century saw the dawn of a new kind of interest and appreciation for Missouri caves. What began to change was public attitudes and perspectives toward cave resources. Some of this came about because of the emergence of the show cave industry.

Show cave owners did not use and abuse the resource. They *exhibited* the resource, calling attention to the natural beauty and mystique of caves. Here was indescribable beauty that should be cherished, beauty created by underground water flow over unthinkable amounts of geologic time. Because of variations in their floor plans and the arrangements of their natural features, no two caves are alike in their appearance, and each is unique with its own personality. It was realized that caves were millions of years old, and rather than being inexhaustible and indestructible, they were fragile and finite.

The exhibition of show caves generated a groundswell of unanswered questions about how, why, and when the caves had been formed. For example, why were some of the animals seen in caves white and blind, while others were as colorful and keen-sighted as animals found above ground? And how many caves did Missouri have? Where were they located? How big were they? How deep into the earth did they penetrate? What was the relationship between individual caves and between caves and springs? And where did the water boiling to the surface in giant cave springs of the Missouri Ozarks come from?

The emergence of the show cave industry had also proven that caves have educational value as natural history museums. Show caves promote tourism, provide jobs, introduce people to caves, and generate dollars for the state's economy. The recreational value of caves had certainly been made apparent during the 1890s and early 1900s.

Missourians recognized that caves were historically important because they had been so useful to American and European settlers in the Ozarks. Throughout the nineteenth century, caves had been used in many different ways to sustain and enhance domestic life in the region. Major advances in cultural anthropology and archaeology also brought a new understanding to the significance of the Native American artifacts and burials sites in Missouri caves.

Professional biologists made their first trips into Ozark caves in the 1880s and 1890s. Ruth Hoppin was the first to describe the blind cave fish that inhabit some Missouri cave streams, while Edward Drinker Cope described blind salamanders. In 1926, the American Museum of Natural History's chair of herpetology, G. Kingsley Noble, explored a number of Missouri caves to study blind salamanders, and in the 1930s and early 1940s, Charles Moore and Carl Hubbs described blind crayfish.

In the 1920s and 1930s, Alfred Burrill, curator of the Capitol museum in Jefferson City, began collecting information about Missouri caves. He was particularly interested in show caves and archaeological sites. His displays at the state Capitol building created a great deal of curiosity about Missouri caves among museum visitors.

Burrill compiled one of the first listings of caves in Missouri, but his list was very short, containing only seventeen caves, which he called "Missouri's better known and developed caverns." All of the caves listed were show caves. "It is hoped that the result of making this partial list available to the general public may result in more caves being opened to visitors and the preserving of some of them for scientific study and the interest of tourists," he said.

In the 1930s, Noel Hubbard, an assistant registrar at the Missouri School of Mines in Rolla (now Missouri University of Science and Technology), became interested in caves. He later organized a caving club on the campus, and by 1949 the Missouri School of Mines Spelunkers (MSM Spelunkers) became an official school club, with a faculty sponsor. Among the members was Willard Farrar, a young geologist who later became the first person to develop a catalog of Missouri caves, both commercial and wild. The MSM Spelunkers became the first organized caving group in Missouri whose goals and organizational structure were consistent with today's definition for an organized caving group.

Also in the 1930s, William Morris Davis published a paper titled "The Origin of Limestone Caverns" in the *Geological Society of America Bulletin,* in which he challenged the accepted theory of geologic textbooks that limestone caverns are formed above the water table in the "vadose zone" of bedrock layers. This is the zone of aerated soil, loose material, and bedrock between the surface and the water table. Below the water table, all layers of bedrock are water-saturated, and this area is called the "phreatic zone." It was his conclusion that caves were formed by water circulating in the phreatic zone, not the vadose zone.

Inspired by Davis's theory, Dr. J Harlen Bretz, a prominent geologist at the University of Chicago, set about in 1947 to test the Davis hypothesis by conducting fieldwork in the caves of the Ozark region of southern Missouri. Bretz proved, to his satisfaction, that Davis was correct and also took up the challenge of determining the geologic history of the Ozark Plateau. Bretz was a great teacher and a challenging geologist with a fine sense of humor. His parents did not give him a first name, so he added a *J* before Harlen. Since it is not an abbreviation, no punctuation is needed. "Throughout all my life," he said. "I have fought typists and printers to leave off that damned period."

In the meantime, in 1953, Dr. Oscar Hawksley, a biology professor at Central Missouri State College (now Central Missouri State University) in Warrensburg, and faculty advisor for the college Outing Club, began corresponding with officials of the National Speleological Society (NSS). The NSS had been founded in 1941, the first national organization established for the exploration and study of caves. In 1954, Hawksley's interest resulted in the founding of the Western Missouri Grotto (WMO Grotto), a chapter of the NSS at Warrensburg.

At first, the membership of the WMO Grotto was drawn from the college Outing Club, but it soon attracted members from throughout the state. Since caves are few and far between in the Warrensburg area, the new grotto did most of its caving in the Ozark region.

Two of the early members of WMO were Jerry Vineyard, then a graduate geology student at the University of Missouri–Columbia, and Frank Dahlgren, a metalworker in St. Louis. In 1956, Hawksley, Vineyard, and Dahlgren attended the NSS Convention in Nashville, Tennessee. Inspired by what they learned and encouraged by the NSS, they returned home to establish the Missouri Speleological Survey (MSS). The goal of the organization was to locate, record, explore, map, and study the caves of Missouri.

Fortuitously, the book *Caves of Missouri,* by J Harlen Bretz, was published in 1956 just as the MSS was being founded. Bretz's book explained his theory for the origin of Missouri caves and quickly became a classic. His work inspired the members of the new cave organization and became one of the catalysts for organized caving in Missouri.

For the first time in Missouri history, caves of the state had a band of admirers who were seriously interested in them for reasons other than to plunder them for their resources or use them for a purpose other than study and preservation.

16

Organized Caving

It often happens the local people don't know what exists in
their own county as only the most daring venture into unlighted
caves. If the entire data on Missouri caves can be gathered, it
will some day make a very readable book of reference for
tourists and citizens.
                          —A. C. Burrill, *Missouri Cave Remains:*
                          A Wonderland with Records of Ancient Life, 1925

There are many kinds of geologic wonders and curiosities in
Missouri such as lost hills, knobs, shut-ins, waterfalls, bluffs,
sinkholes, springs, and caves. Yet it was not until the second decade
of the twentieth century that some Missourians began to recognize
the need to protect outstanding examples of these geographic features. In 1913, Governor Herbert Hadley recommended the
appointment of a legislative commission to select some of the natural wonders and beauties of the state for purchase as parks. He envi-
sioned a "chain of parks" across the Ozarks.

Among the first geologic wonders selected and proposed to the
General Assembly was Onondaga Cave, near Leasburg in Crawford
County, and Ha Ha Tonka, in Camden County. Ha Ha Tonka is one
of Missouri's most outstanding examples of cave and karst topography. Unfortunately there was no money available for creating state
parks. A bill was passed in 1917 setting aside a percentage of game
and fish receipts for a state park fund, but it was not until 1924 that
the state began acquiring land in the Ozarks for parks. The acquisitions targeted historic sites and tracts of land that contained large

springs. The one exception was the creation of Meramec State Park in Franklin County. There are thirty-eight caves in the park. "These 7,000 acres of wilderness provide one of Missouri's cavelands," reported a state publication in 1929. So the state's involvement with caves actually began before the creation of any organized caving groups in Missouri whose interest in caves was more academic than recreational.

In 1936, Missouri created its Department of Conservation. The agency began working in 1937 and teamed up with the Civilian Conservation Corps (CCC) to restock wildlife in the Ozarks, plant trees, and build dams, roads, and recreational areas. At Meramec State Park, the CCC made significant improvements to Fisher Cave, which was the park's signature show cave.

In 1933, Missouri passed legislation enabling the U.S. Forest Service to start defining areas for a national forest. By 1945, the Forest Service had created the Mark Twain National Forest, mostly in southern Missouri. Its 1.25 million acres contains hundreds of caves, but no effort was made to inventory or study the cave resources. It would be decades before true cave resource management would begin in the Mark Twain National Forest.

By 1956, no one had any idea how many caves were on land owned, leased, or managed in Missouri by federal or state agencies. Nor did anyone have the foggiest notion how many caves might be on privately owned land. One early estimate was that Missouri might have as many as one thousand caves, but it was just a guess.

This was the situation in the fall of 1956, when the Missouri Speleological Survey was created. It was the first and remains the only private statewide organization in Missouri whose goals are to locate, record, explore, map, and study the caves of the state. The MSS is a nonprofit organization that unites the cave-oriented ambitions, skills, knowledge, enthusiasm, and dedication of both amateurs and professionals. Its membership is open to anyone who demonstrates responsibility in cave conservation and who cooperates with the MSS in its effort to achieve its goals. Its work is largely carried on by the organized caving groups of Missouri who sit on the MSS board of directors.

To facilitate its work and provide a permanent repository for

The three founders of the Missouri Speleological Survey, Inc., left to right, Frank Dahlgren, Dr. Oscar Hawksley, and Jerry D. Vineyard, on the steps of the Missouri Department of Natural Resources, Division of Geology and Land Survey, Rolla, Missouri, celebrating the recording of Missouri's five-thousandth cave. (Photo by H. Dwight Weaver, 1990)

material gathered by the affiliate caving groups, the MSS entered into a cooperative agreement with the Missouri Geological Survey and Water Resources (now the Missouri Department of Natural Resources Division of Geology and Land Survey). Former state geologist Thomas Beveridge extended a hand of friendship to the cavers right from the beginning. It was a handshake that would bear fruit and foster a partnership that has lasted for more than fifty years and hopefully will last for generations to come.

Since the MSS was a fledgling private organization in 1956 with no permanent headquarters and no start-up funding, the Missouri Geological Survey agreed to be a repository for all Missouri cave maps and reports and agreed to reproduce cave maps for the MSS. It was mutually beneficial, since the geological survey needed the cave information that the MSS would be providing.

The accomplishments of the MSS since 1956 toward fostering a better understanding and appreciation for Missouri caves are considerable. For instance, starting with a list of only 437 known caves in the state when it was founded, the MSS has added caves to that list at the rate of more than 120 caves per year for the past fifty years. There are now more than 6,200 known caves in Missouri, and as the hunt for more continues, the statistics change on an almost weekly basis.

In the 1960s, Congress established the Ozark National Scenic Riverways in Dent, Shannon, and Carter counties. It was the first national scenic riverway and subsequently influenced the establishment of the Eleven Point National Scenic River in Oregon County. The National Park Service soon discovered there were hundreds of caves on these properties in need of special attention.

Also in the 1960s, the MSS took a stand opposing the construction of the Meramec Park Dam by the U.S. Army Corps of Engineers, which would have resulted in the inundation of scores of caves in the Meramec River valley. The valley has a high density of caves. Several of the caves possess unique formations and provide habitat for rare forms of life, including endangered species of bats. The MSS was one of many groups and organizations that opposed the project, which was eventually defeated.

In the 1970s, the conservation department, influenced by endangered species laws, threats to habitat by proposed dams that might inundate caves, several major bat studies, and the creation of the Natural History Section in the Missouri Department of Conservation, began acquiring numerous tracts of land to preserve forest and wildlife resources and protect threatened and endangered species. In the late 1970s, the department began specifically targeting cave resources. Early acquisitions included Bat Cave in Miller County, Powder Mill Creek Cave in Shannon County, Coffin Cave in Laclede County, Smittle Cave in Wright County, and Great Spirit Cave in Pulaski County. The Department of Conservation currently owns 236 Missouri caves. With government agencies acquiring significant karst areas of the state, an imperative was born to protect and manage cave resources with conservation and preservation in mind.

Conservationists discovered that Missouri caves are the habitat for rare and delicate life forms, contain invaluable prehistoric human and extinct ice age animal materials, and are ornamented with beautiful, unique, fragile cave formations. They also contain vast reservoirs of water and are sensitive components of the major spring systems and groundwater aquifers of the Ozarks. In 1980, the Missouri Cave Resources Act was passed. It protects caves by prohibiting vandalism of any type and recognizes the value of caves. It also maintains the right of private cave owners to manage or use their cave as they see fit. The law also helps protect the quality of Missouri's groundwater by prohibiting the use of a cave or spring for sewage disposal or other pollution-causing activities.

In the late 1960s and 1970s, the Department of Natural Resources Division of State Parks began adding parks to its system where karst and caves were a focus of interpretation and visitation. Examples include Rock Bridge Memorial State Park, in Boone County south of Columbia, and Ha Ha Tonka State Park, near Camdenton in Camden County. There are more than 120 caves in sixteen state parks administered by the Missouri Department of Natural Resources.

By the early 1980s, under contractual agreements, members of the MSS and Cave Research Foundation, a private research group, teamed up to inventory cave resources on government lands in Missouri, so the agencies could make wise decisions in the development of their cave management plans. The agencies own about 1,500 of the more than 6,200 caves recorded in the state.

In 1985, the MSS received the silver medal of the President's Volunteer Action Award. The award was presented at the White House by President Ronald Reagan and was accepted on behalf of the MSS by H. Dwight Weaver and Gregory J. "Tex" Yokum. The MSS is the only caving organization in the United States ever to win such an award and to be recognized by a sitting U.S. president for its work in documenting the cave resources of a state.

In 1993, the cavers of Missouri took a bold step into the future by organizing the Missouri Caves and Karst Conservancy (MCKC) with the help of the Ozark Regional Land Trust (ORLT). Today, in

On behalf of the Missouri Speleological Survey, Inc., Dwight Weaver accepts the 1985 Presidential Action Award from President Ronald Reagan at the White House in Washington, D.C. (Official White House photograph, April 1985)

partnership with ORLT, the MSS, state agencies, and several caving clubs, the MCKC is helping to protect the endangered Ozark cave fish and is managing several wild caves that need special protection; the organizations have become cave owners themselves.

If the cavers of Missouri have learned anything at all over the past fifty years of intense cave recording, mapping, and data collection, it is that our caves deserve protection. Since the early nineteenth century, our remarkable cave resources have been put to many uses in serving the people of the state. But only since the 1950s have caves been recognized to have importance well beyond that of providing some service or materials useful to individuals and society. Today, we realize that caves are unique features of our landscape.

Considering their age and their very existence, they merit respect. They are nonrenewable, irreplaceable natural resources and should be wisely managed and preserved for all future generations of Missourians to enjoy and cherish.

17

The Mystique of Caves

There is an odd belief that stalactites and stalagmites are some-
how deadlier than any other stones, and that even a slight blow
from a piece of "drip rock" is generally fatal.
—VANCE RANDOLPH, *Ozark Superstitions,* 1947

Why is it that some people find caves absolutely irresistible,
while others avoid caves entirely and would just as soon not
even think about them?

When mountain climbers are asked why they climb mountains,
they stereotypically reply, "Because they are there." Some may think
an interest in caves can be explained in the same way, but it is not
that simple.

For most of history, humans not only feared the unknown but also
shunned it. For thousands of years, humanity stood in awe of mountain peaks, glaciers, caves, and all remote places. The unknown and
the forbidden were viewed as much the same thing. It was not until
the 1700s that Europeans began to make a popular adventure out of
scaling mountains. And it was not until the late 1800s that Americans began to explore caves as a recreational activity. The science of
caves, or "speleology," was not born until the twentieth century.

Humans were slow to explore the unknown underground because
it was thought to be the realm of devils and death. An account of the
discovery of Marvel Cave published in 1915 said the following:

Hunters and settlers visited Roark Peak before the Civil War.
They crawled down the craterlike depression . . . and leaned

over the edges of the long, narrow gap in the rock bottom of the crater. They looked down into a hole, which seemed at first to have neither sides nor bottom. It was without form and void. Strange noises came to strained ears. Imaginations helped eyes to see gleams of light and shadowy forms. "The Devil's Den" these early settlers called it. A closer acquaintance with his satanic majesty was not sought by them.

In *Innocents Abroad*, published in 1869, Mark Twain wrote, "The memory of a cave I used to know at home was always in my mind, with its lofty passages, its silence and solitude, its shrouding gloom, its sepulchral echoes, its flitting lights, and more than all, its sudden revelations of branching crevices and corridors where we least expected them."

Note the descriptive words: "without form and void," "strange noises," "gleams of light," "silence and solitude," and "shrouding gloom." These are aspects of caves that stir the imagination, play upon human fears, tap into religious myths, bare unexpected human weaknesses, whet unsuspecting appetites, and make seductive promises or threats about the unseen and the unknown.

Wild caves, where there are no trails or electric lights and where nature reigns supreme, are more than just gloomy places shrouded in darkness. They are special places that harbor an unusual blend of natural elements capable of producing a unique underground experience. It is, above all else, the sensory aura of caves that repels many people yet proves irresistible to others.

The underground setting also promises the rewards of discovery, information, and knowledge to those brave enough to probe its dark hidden recesses and determined enough to overcome the obstacles it presents to challenge human endurance, competence, and innovation.

Caves do all of this under a cover of darkness. They reach out and touch all the human senses. Missouri cave air is heavy with moisture and penetrates clothing with a chill. The cave smells earthy, raw, primitive. It seems that you can almost taste a cave sometimes, because its atmosphere is so rich in earthy substances.

When you approach a cave in the summer, the first thing you

Caver Travis Zumwalt prepares for his journey into the darkness of a Missouri cave. (Photo by H. Dwight Weaver, 1995)

sense is this earthy, basementlike smell and the chill of the cave air. In winter, these senses are not activated so quickly upon approaching the cave but are evident soon after entry. Many people find these two elements an uncomfortable combination. Both sensations are associated with the underground, darkness, and death.

In a cave you can easily hear things unseen, unknown, and imaginary because of heightened emotions and sensitivities. These sounds are generally caused by the movement of water, shifting sediments, airflow, and cave life. A cave seems to amplify some sounds and distort others. Out of that blackness comes muffled plops, titters and squeaks, rumbles, muted roars, faint moans, breathy whispering sounds, scraping sounds, and even voices. Your imagination sometimes makes it possible for you to hear distant human voices even in deep, remote underground passages where no human has ever been before. Spirits never seen but often heard seem to haunt some caves. Cave exploration is not for the faint of heart.

Caving is a contact activity, an adventure in constantly changing textures—rough, gritty, smooth, wet, slippery, and sticky. The waters of cave streams and underground pools slither about you like a snake. Mud sucks at your feet like a demon. Shifting wet sand and other sediments feel almost seductive if you have to crawl in them.

Cave exploration is a journey into the earth. It is a penetration of the severed limestone arteries that riddle the skin of the Ozarks. Caves are networks of natural veins that transport groundwater, the life-giving bloodstream of nature. In the underground there dwells an alien that can scare the living daylights out of anyone who is insecure in shadowy surroundings. That alien's name is Total Darkness.

Total darkness fills every chamber, corridor, and cranny beyond the twilight zone of a cave entrance. It is not unlike a black liquid. It exhibits qualities that are as substantive as a living creature. It can be friendly or frightening, comforting or irritating, all depending upon your frame of mind and the circumstances. It can even be hostile and dangerous. It is a creature cavers flirt with constantly and it is kept at bay only by the artificial light a caver carries.

The lights cavers have to use are finite. While ocean divers are limited by the amount of air their tanks can carry, cavers are limited by the amount of light their equipment can store and discharge.

As you make your way through a wild cave, guided by your fragile light, the blackness shrinks away like a frightened animal. Your light stabs it, breaking it into lurking shadows. The darkness has a life of its own. It stalks you. It crawls and creeps around you as you move. At every opportunity it seems to sweep up and cling to your back. You actually feel it sometimes. It is there with you at all times, unrelenting and unforgiving. And it waits, patiently. Extinguish your light, and it descends like a blanket, so thick, so deep, it robs you of all sight and sense of reality.

These are the elements of the underground mystique. They are elements that cavers live and cope with every second they spend underground. It is the cavers' ability to cope with these elements rationally that makes cavers different.

It has been said, "Forces at work since the founding of our nation have tempted us to give up our exploring, or leave it to marginal men and women." For cavers, this margin is the edge of discovery. Modern science was born in the exploring spirit. It helps us determine how much of our world is yet unknown. For the caver, the search for the unknown and the unsolved mysteries of caves are the heart and soul of the underground mystique.

The Twelve Cave Regions of Missouri

Introduction

"Missouri has been called a 'Cave Factory' because the region is now undergoing perhaps the most intense episode of cave making in its entire geologic history," says cave authority Jerry Vineyard. This is happening because the bedrock of the mountainlike region is a mixture of reasonably thick limestone and dolomite bedrock formations that can be slowly dissolved by groundwater. The region also has a temperate climate, is well vegetated, and has about forty inches of rainfall each year. This permits the groundwater to become charged with carbonic acid, the agent that makes it possible for the water to dissolve various mineral components within the bedrock, calcium carbonate in particular.

The cave-making process has been under way for tens of millions of years, and some of the oldest caves are thought to be the deeply buried cave systems that are currently full of water and discharging that water to create the giant springs of the Ozarks. Some of these water-filled caves are two hundred to three hundred feet below the mouth of the springs where the water comes to the surface in Ozark valleys.

Air-filled caves that riddle the hills of the Ozarks are also ancient by our reckoning of time. They have been made accessible by surface erosion and by streams that have carved out deep valleys, creating hills, bluffs, and ridges. This process has cut the landscape and caves apart, creating entrances and spring outlets. The erosion process also lowered the water table in the hills, allowing the caves to be drained during their water-filled stage of development and permitting air to fill them. Many of the caves became air-filled hundreds of thousands of years ago, perhaps as many as one or two million years ago. Since then, stalactites, stalagmites, and other cave formations have been deposited inside the caves by mineral-laden groundwater seeping, dripping, and flowing into the underground chambers and passageways. Surface streams that have invaded the caves since they became air-filled have also deposited great amounts of sand, gravel, clay, and other sediments, although some sediments in the caves originated when the caves were water-filled and in their earlier stages of development.

Groundwater entering the joints and crevices of the bedrock always seeks a lower level, and in so doing it often carries soils from the surface, which in some areas creates bowl-shaped or funnel-shaped depressions called sinkholes. Sinkholes feed groundwater into cave systems and sometimes actually breach cave ceilings to create entrances or pits at the bottom of the sinkholes. Any landscape that is characterized by the presence of springs, caves, sinkholes, and streams that disappear into the ground is called "karst topography." Much of the Ozark region is considered a karst area. In some locations, there are so many sinkholes that they themselves create the hilly landscape, such as that near Pierpont in Boone County, on the northern fringe of the Ozarks; around Perryville in Perry County, on the eastern fringe of the Ozarks; in the Ha Ha Tonka and Montreal areas of Camden County; and in the West Plains and Thayer areas of Howell and Oregon counties.

There are many varieties of limestone and dolomite formations, each group having its own unique combination of characteristics. Mixed in with the limestone are other types of rocks and minerals that add to the complexity of the structure. Joints, which are the vertical cracks in the bedrock, and bedding planes, which are the horizontal meeting points between layers of bedrock, are the arteries that give groundwater access to the bedrock. Millions of different combinations of these structural elements result in uncountable combinations of interesting cave features, which is why no two caves look alike in their floor plans and have varied collections of water-deposited and water-sculptured natural wonders and curiosities.

Missouri caves come in an unbelievable variety of sizes, lengths, and shapes. All caves, regardless of their size, provide a habitat for animal life. Even small caves can be lavishly adorned with cave formations. Fewer than 3 percent of the caves in Missouri exceed a mile in length. The greatest majority of caves in the Ozarks are only a few hundred or few thousand feet in length. Underground chambers range in size from rooms barely large enough to accommodate two or three people, to gargantuan cathedral-like rooms that may be eighty to a hundred feet high, one hundred to three hundred feet wide, and several thousand feet in length.

Not all caves in Missouri are horizontal, particularly those that must be entered through pits. Vertical development, which can create more than one level to a cave, can make exploration difficult. Only a small number of pit caves in Missouri have vertical drops greater than one hundred feet.

Level cave floors are uncommon, which makes walking problematic. The floors of most wild caves are very irregular, cluttered with natural obstructions, slippery, muddy, and wet. To explore almost any cave in the Ozarks for any great length requires getting through water that can be shallow or deep and tromping through quagmires of clay that cling like glue to footwear, clothing, and skin. A caver may have to crawl or squeeze through tight places or crawl along stretches of low-ceiling passage that may be nearly filled with cold water. If a person is bothered even slightly by claustrophobia, caving is not a wise undertaking.

Climbing in caves is always a risky business but is often a requirement for reaching the ultimate goal. If you do not like rock climbing and are afraid of heights, caving may not be your best choice for outdoor adventure. The chilly temperature of the cave is not going to vary and neither will the temperature of the water, meaning that in Missouri hypothermia is always a risk in caving and the caver must be properly attired and equipped for such conditions. Total darkness is the ever-present condition in Missouri's chilly, wet caves. Having adequate light and three or more dependable sources of light for each member of the party could mean the difference between life or death. Lose your light in a cave, and you are in serious trouble.

The cave regions of Missouri. (Map by Susan Ferber)

The greatest dangers in Missouri caving is loss of light, flash flooding, and serious injury from a fall. To avoid these hazards, cavers
always inform family or other cavers when and where they are going
underground and when they expect to be out so that if they fail to
appear within a reasonable time, a rescue can be undertaken. They
do not go caving when thunderstorms and heavy rain are possible—
some caves may collect their water from distances as far as forty
miles away and flash flood. Proper equipment, teamwork, caution,
experience, and good judgment go a long way toward preventing
serious injury or death.

There have been deaths in Missouri caves attributed to all of
these causes and others, but it is uncommon for serious accidents
to happen to members of the organized caving community because
of training, teamwork, and experience. It is the organized cavers

who are often called upon to perform cave rescues when they are necessary. No one should go caving alone or without wearing a hard hat. And it is wise to have at least one or more experienced cavers in the team.

The following is a brief overview of the cave resources in twelve Missouri regions and covers all of the counties in Missouri that currently have recorded caves.

Dad Truitt Cave Region

The three Missouri counties that constitute the Dad Truitt Cave Region cover 1,900 square miles. A total of 190 caves were recorded here as of April 2007. The cave count, by county, is Jasper, 26; McDonald, 106; and Newton, 58.

The land in this region is scenic Ozark country in the middle of the Springfield Plain and has a great diversity of landscape features ranging from the prairies of Jasper County to the rugged hills of McDonald County.

Tourism is a vintage industry here. J. A. "Dad" Truitt, the "Caveman of the Ozarks," explored and developed most of the region's show caves between 1916 and 1940. The show caves of this region have included Bluff Dwellers Cave, Crystal Cave, Mt. Shira Cave, Ozark Wonder Cave, Truitt's Cave, and Wind Cave.

Jasper and Newton counties were at the heart of the Tri-State Lead-Zinc District from 1848 to the 1960s. When the lead mining industry was at its peak, prospectors and miners sometimes converted caves into temporary homes.

In the 1890s, miners discovered a one-room air-filled cave lined with crystals beneath the city of Joplin. They named it Crystal Cave. Groundwater pumping that had been necessary for mining had lowered the water table, emptying the void of its former water-filled condition. "The entire surface of the cave, top, sides, and bottom, is lined with calcite crystals, so closely packed together as to form a continuous sheet, and most of them of great size . . . as much as two feet long," said geologist Arthur Winslow in 1894. The cave was subsequently opened to the public. It remained open for a decade. When mining played out and groundwater pumping ceased, the water table rebounded and the cave refilled with water, ending its days as a show cave.

In recent years, caving biologists have discovered that some caves of the region provide a habitat used by three endangered species—gray bats, the Ozark blind cavefish, and the bristly crayfish. Steps have been taken to protect the caves that harbor these fascinating creatures.

Daniel Boone Cave Region

The ten Missouri counties that constitute the Daniel Boone Cave Region cover 5,479 square miles. A total of 222 caves were recorded here as of April 2007. The cave count, by county, is Boone, 108; Callaway, 17; Cooper, 12; Gasconade, 10; Howard, 5; Moniteau, 36; Montgomery, 8; Randolph, 6; Saline, 4; and Warren, 16.

The land of this region stretches from the saline springs of Howard and Saline counties, which were developed by the sons of Daniel Boone, to the eastern edge of Warren County, where Daniel Boone's grave is located.

The Missouri River meanders through the region. Running back from the river bottom for several miles are rugged hills and hollows where, in some locations, remarkable sandstone caves are located. The best examples are Graham Cave, in Graham Cave State Park in Montgomery County, and Arnold Research Cave, in Callaway County. Both caves are archaeologically significant.

Intriguing sandstone caves can also be found elsewhere, and rare dark zone rock art has been found in one of these caves. The whole of Warren County, which has several interesting sandstone caves, seems to be riddled with cave lore, most of it having been thoroughly checked out by cavers and found to be more fiction than fact.

On the uplands bordering the Missouri River in Boone, Cooper, and Moniteau counties there are well-developed sinkhole plains noted for caves that can only be entered through sinkhole pits and that drop fifty to one hundred feet. There are also extensive cave systems like the Devil's Icebox in Rock Bridge Memorial State Park near Columbia. The Devil's Icebox is the most extensive cave of the region, having more than six miles of charted underground passages. It is one of the most significant caves in the state.

Ranking second in the region for length and popularity is Hunter's Cave in the Three Creeks Conservation Area, which is now a preserve for endangered gray bats.

Several caves of the region have yielded ice age animal remains and are important for their fossil resources. Caves of the area are also a habitat for endangered species, such as the gray bat and the pink planarian, the latter an extremely rare type of flatworm found only in the Devil's Icebox.

Rocheport Cave, a few miles west of Columbia where Interstate 70 crosses the Missouri River, is a prominent gray bat preserve managed by the Missouri Department of Conservation. In the 1960s it was a privately owned show cave called Boone Cave. Although the public is no longer permitted to wander the corridors of Boone Cave, braver souls can enjoy special adventure trips in the Devil's Icebox.

Heart of the Ozarks Cave Region

The eight Missouri counties that constitute the Heart of the Ozarks Cave Region cover 6,237 square miles. A total of 1,062 caves were recorded here as of April 2007. The cave count, by county, is Douglas, 107; Howell, 40; Laclede, 80; Ozark, 82; Phelps, 151; Pulaski, 358; Texas, 182; and Wright, 62.

Most of the land in this region is rugged, rocky, picturesque hill country abounding in spring-fed streams and rivers. Among the more than one thousand caves known in these hills are many of state's most important and beautiful caves.

Many caves feature huge underground chambers, multiple levels, rushing cave streams, and thundering waterfalls. Caves 1,500 to 5,000 feet in length are common. Ten caves have been surveyed for over one mile, and several exceed two miles. Piquet Cave now has nearly five miles of charted passage. Continued survey work will undoubtedly add many miles to the cave systems of the Heart of the Ozarks area.

Most of the caves in this region have their entrances in bluffs and on hillsides, but there are also pit caves that drop seventy to one hundred feet. Buzzard Cave in Wright County has a series of vertical drops that help the cave reach a total depth of 308 feet. It is Missouri's second deepest cave, second in depth only to Marvel Cave in Stone County.

Saltpeter and onyx miners left their scars in these caves but overlooked fabulous beauty. Hidden away are massive columns, lavish displays of stalactites and stalagmites, blankets of glittering flowstone, and deposits of anthodites, cave pearls, boxwork, rimstone dams, and moonmilk. It is no wonder that three of the area's caves became show caves for a time—Onyx Mountain Caverns (Onyx Cave), Great Spirit Cave (Inca Cave), and Roubidoux Cave (Indian Cave).

Archaeologists have worked these caves for nearly a century and found plenty, including Indian burials. Paleontologists have also wandered these caves in search of ancient animal bones. They've been successful; the caves have yielded, among other species, the remains of ice age jaguars, short-faced bears, peccary, and ground sloth.

This is the land of the endangered gray and Indiana bats. More than thirty caves shelter these fragile creatures. The gray bats use quite a few of the caves for hibernating and rearing their young, while the Indiana bats use the caves mainly for hibernation.

Kansas City Cave Region

The seven Missouri counties that constitute the Kansas City Cave Region cover 4,253 square miles. A total of 20 caves were recorded here as of April 2007. The cave count, by county, is Cass, 2; Clay, 1; Jackson, 8; Johnson, 2; Lafayette, 1; Pettis, 5; and Platte, 1. While there are very few natural caves in this region, there are many underground limestone quarries in the Kansas City area in the Bethany Falls Limestone formation. Some have been converted into underground warehouses and put to other commercial uses. People sometimes mistake these old quarries for natural caves.

The premier caves of Jackson County are Unity Natural Tunnel, Harrison Parkway Cave, and Santa Fe Trail Spring Cave. Unity Natural Tunnel is 125 feet long, 25 feet wide, and 8 feet high. In 1906, George Pierson mapped Harrison Parkway Cave; this cave is about 140 feet long. Pierson's map is the second oldest cave map on record in the Missouri cave files, second only to the map of Marvel Cave created in the late 1800s by S. F. Prince. Santa Fe Trail Spring Cave is of historic interest because it once issued a good spring that provided water for traders and immigrants headed west on the Santa Fe Trail.

Mark Twain Cave Region

The seven Missouri counties that constitute the Mark Twain Cave Region cover 3,796 square miles. A total of 139 caves were recorded here as of April 2007. The cave count, by county, is Knox, 2; Lincoln, 36; Marion, 17; Monroe, 2; Pike, 38; Ralls, 43; and Shelby, 1.

This region is endowed with the romance of Tom Sawyer, Huck Finn, Becky Thatcher, and Injun Joe, all of them fictional, but the cave where their make-believe adventures took place is very real. It is, in fact, one of the most remarkable labyrinthine caves in the Midwest and has almost three miles of confusing, intersecting passages.

In the hill opposite Mark Twain Cave is Cameron Cave, another maze cave with nearly five miles of surveyed passage. To the southeast, barely across the Marion County line into Ralls County, is La Baume Cave, a maze cave with nearly two miles of surveyed passage. And to the northwest, within the city limits of Hannibal, is Murphy Cave, a maze cave with two miles of surveyed passage.

The maze caves are formed in a belt of Louisiana limestone that has an unusual geologic history. Outside of this belt, which has severely limited boundaries, the caves of the region are more conventional in floor plan and extent. Most of the caves outside the belt are small, but Buzzard Cave in Pike County has more than one mile of surveyed passage.

Gray bats have found a home here, protected by three caves in

Pike and Ralls counties. There are also several pit caves, one in Lincoln County that drops eighty feet, and one in Ralls County that plunges fifty feet. Another pit cave has yielded the ancient remains of black bear and bobcat.

Meramec River Cave Region

The three Missouri counties that constitute the Meramec River Cave Region cover 2,356 square miles. A total of 395 caves were recorded here as of April 2007. The cave count, by county, is Crawford, 214; Franklin, 100; and Washington, 81.

The Meramec River has nearly one hundred miles of fast-flowing, floatable water in this region bordered by majestic bluffs and rugged hills where caves and springs abound. The caves are endowed with size, length, and grandeur, which is why four of Missouri's more outstanding show caves are found here—Cathedral Cave, Fisher Cave, Meramec Caverns, and Onondaga Cave. They've been show caves for many decades and are still attracting tens of thousands of visitors each year. All four caves are noted for their gigantic underground chambers festooned with impressive and unforgettable assemblages of cave formations.

Cavers have done a lot of mapping in this region. There are at least seven caves that have a combined total of more than eleven miles of surveyed passage. Among the wild caves noted for their length and beauty are Great Scott Cave, Hamilton Cave, Nameless Cave, Moore's Cave, Jagged Canyon Cave, and Estes Cave. The wild caves of this region feature scenic entrances, multiple levels, deep canyons, high domes, waterfalls, underground lakes, and enough history to intrigue and please any history buff.

Meriwether Lewis and William Clark visited Tavern Cave in Franklin County early in their historic expedition. One cave in the area contains rare tabular barite crystals the size of basketballs. Another has astonishing helictite bushes, a most uncommon type of cave formation. Onyx miners plundered some of the beauty here a century ago.

And of course, bats know good caves when they see them, and

they've taken refuge here. Endangered gray bats use quite a few caves in this area.

Old Settlements Cave Region

The nine Missouri counties that constitute the Old Settlements Cave Region cover 4,758 square miles. A total of 852 caves were recorded here as of April 2007. The cave count, by county, is Bollinger, 4; Cape Girardeau, 42; Iron, 26; Madison, 21; Perry, 659; Scott, 3; Ste. Genevieve, 73; St. Francois, 21; and Stoddard, 3.

This region is where white settlement first took root west of the Mississippi River. The French explored and settled here in the 1720s and opened the state's first lead mines.

Caves are plentiful in the northern half and central zone of the Old Settlements Cave Region but play out quickly in the southern extremities as the area approaches the lowlands of the Missouri Bootheel. Only a few small caves are found in Bollinger, Scott, and Stoddard counties. Caves are larger and more extensive in Cape Girardeau, Madison, and St. Francois counties but are still modest in size compared to most caves throughout the Ozarks. Iron County has the only cave in this region where endangered bats have taken up residence—Indiana bats use the cave as a hibernaculum.

For Ste. Genevieve and Perry counties, it is a whole different story when it comes to caves, especially Perry. Here, the landscape sometimes appears to have literally "caved in" because of overlapping sinkholes. Cave passages honeycomb the bedrock. There are more caves per square mile in Perry County than in any other county of the state. It may be the most cavernous county in North America. Perryville has more than forty-five known caves just within its city limits.

At present, Perry County has 659 recorded caves, and the number keeps climbing. For the past forty years, Missouri cavers have been methodically surveying this dark and forbidding underworld and have charted more than 150 miles of cave passages. Among the most extensive caves of the county are Berome Moore Cave, Lost and Found Cave, Meisner Crevice, Mertz Cave, Mystery-Rimstone Cave, Snow Caverns, Hot Caverns, and Zahner Cave.

Pit caves are common in this region, and their shafts sometimes appear bottomless. Among the deepest pit caves are Fantastic Pit at 106 feet and Echo Pit at 120 feet. Elsewhere pits ranging from 40 to 80 feet deep in a single vertical drop are fairly common.

Many of the caves of Perry County contain beautiful features that include rimstone dams, waterfalls, banded travertine, picturesque gypsum formations, and massive flowstone curtains. One cave of this region has one of the state's largest stalagmites.

The caves are also water sculpted with stunning scenic underground arches and natural bridges, fluted pit walls, and scalloped, Swiss cheese–like bedrock. Ice age animals walked the dark corridors of these caves or fell into pits and died here tens of thousands of years ago, leaving behind their bones and tracks.

Osage River Cave Region

The ten counties that constitute the Osage River Cave region cover 5,900 square miles. A total of 485 caves were recorded here as of April 2007. The cave count, by county, is Benton, 42; Camden, 166; Cole, 21; Henry, 22; Hickory, 21; Maries, 36; Miller, 63; Morgan, 30; Osage, 21; and St. Clair, 63.

The Osage River valley is noted for its two giant man-made lakes—Lake of the Ozarks behind Bagnell Dam, and the Harry S. Truman Reservoir behind Truman Dam.

The Lake of the Ozarks was created in 1931 and Truman Reservoir in 1979. Both lakes inundated caves; however, the caves flooded by Truman Reservoir are small. They were recorded and studied before the lake was formed. The caves beneath Lake of the Ozarks unfortunately were not so small and not carefully researched. The Lake of the Ozarks was formed before caves were considered important enough to record, map, and study. No one knows how many caves lie beneath the surface of the lake, but considering the cavernous nature of the basin area, there may be more than one hundred inundated caves. Several were noted for their large chambers, history, length, and beautiful formations.

The caves of Benton, Cole, Henry, Hickory, Maries, Osage, and St.

Clair counties are relatively small but not in every case insignificant because many of them are habitats for gray and Indiana bats.

There is a cluster of bluff caves at Monegaw in St. Clair County that are rich in outlaw history of the 1870s because this locale was frequented by the James and Younger gangs. Cleveland Cave in St. Clair County and River Cave in Osage County were show caves early in the twentieth century. Hickory County has two caves that were mined for barite in the 1930s.

The creation of the Lake of the Ozarks stimulated show cave development here, beginning in the 1930s. Bridal Cave, Jacob's Cave, and Ozark Caverns are still open to the public. Bridal Cave, noted for its beauty and underground weddings, is located right on the shoreline of the lake. Jacob's Cave, noted for its ice age bones and delicate formations, was the first cave opened to the public after the Lake of the Ozarks was formed. Ozark Caverns in Lake of the Ozarks State Park is noted for its exquisite showerhead cave formations.

Other caves once commercial in this area include Ancient Grotto (Vernon Cave), Arrow Point Cave (Wright Cave), Bunch Cave (Big Niangua Cave), Fantasy World Caverns (Stark Caverns), Flanders Cave, Indian Burial Cave (Big Mouth Cave), and Mystic River Cave (River Cave).

Some caves in this region once served as Indian burial grounds while others were mined for onyx and guano. Caves in the Barnumton area of Camden County once supplied saltpeter for a gunpowder plant on Fiery Forks Creek.

The two most outstanding geologic aspects of this area are in Camden County and feature caves and sinkholes. They are Ha Ha Tonka State Park and Carroll Cave near Montreal. Carroll Cave is world class in size and extent. Survey work underway at the cave has already surpassed twelve miles. The cave has huge chambers and passageways, is more than one level, and features beautiful formations and an underground river that feeds one of the region's large springs.

Riverways Cave Region

The eight Missouri counties that constitute the Riverways Cave

Region cover 5,409 square miles. A total of 997 caves were recorded here as of April 2007. The cave count, by county, is Butler, 6; Carter, 79; Dent, 96; Oregon, 147; Reynolds, 64; Ripley, 12; Shannon, 571; and Wayne, 22.

If there were a Fountain of Youth, it would surely be hidden somewhere in the primeval beauty of the Riverways Cave Region. This is the land of giant cave springs where the earth turns itself inside out and such enormous quantities of cold, fresh, springwater gush forth that four gemstone-clear Ozark rivers have been born—the Current, Black, Jacks Fork, and Eleven Point. The Current and Eleven Point are so highly regarded that they have been designated National Scenic Riverways.

The region is heavily forested, with deep, rugged Ozark valleys where beauty runs wild and the spring caves run deep—so deep, in fact, that some of the spring throats do not bottom out until they've descended three hundred feet into the earth. But between the surface and the spring outlets are sinkhole pits in the hills that open into gigantic underground lakes. The throat in the Devil's Well sinkhole opens to a ninety-five-foot drop into an unbelievably large lake room, where the water itself is one hundred feet deep.

Among the most extensive caves in this region are Round Spring Caverns, a show cave with more than one mile of surveyed passage, and Wind Cave, a wild cave with more than seven thousand feet of passage. But these caves pale in length to Powder Mill Creek Cave in Shannon County; cavers have mapped this cave's awesome innards for seven miles.

In a cavernous region so blessed with underground rivers and lakes, one would expect to find caves with rich ecosystems. Indeed, the southern blind cavefish and the Salem blind crayfish live here, and so do endangered gray and Indiana bats, which use caves in Dent, Oregon, Reynolds, and Shannon counties. The caves in this region harbor great beauty, often in the form of fine displays of helictites, aragonite crystals, cave pearls, massive flowstone, great boxwork, golden calcite, lily pad formations, and remarkably long soda-straw stalactites.

Moonshiners once hid their illegal stills in these caves, and Indian-artifact hunters and buried-treasure seekers left spoil piles from indiscriminate digging. Yet the scars they left mar the beauty of fortunately only a few caves.

This region is noted for show caves, including Devil's Well, Rebel Cave, Emerald Grotto (the Sinks), Cardareva Cave, Lewis Cave, Round Spring Caverns, and Keener Cave. At Keener, dugout canoes that resemble outrigger canoes or French pirogues were brought up from the bottom of an underground lake in the 1930s and 1960s. The whereabouts of these old canoes today is not known.

Two other natural wonders in the Riverways Cave Region must be mentioned—the Grand Gulf in Oregon County and the Gulf in Wayne County. At the Grand Gulf, a great cave system collapsed eons ago, creating one of the largest canyons in the Ozarks. A great natural bridge spans the gulf, and the water that invades this chasm after rains drains into a cave that feeds Mammoth Spring, miles away in Arkansas. And at the Gulf, in Wayne County, in the darkness of a large, one-room cave that can only be entered by boat, rests the deepest underground lake in Missouri. Its water is two hundred feet deep!

Shelter Cave Region

The three Missouri counties that constitute the Shelter Cave Region cover 2,335 square miles. A total of 60 caves were recorded here as of April 2007. The cave count, by county, is Barton, 14; Bates, 5; and Vernon, 41. These counties are along the Missouri-Kansas border, about halfway between Kansas City and Joplin. They feature a rolling landscape mixed with wetlands and tallgrass prairie drained by the Marais des Cygnes, Grand, Little Osage, and Marmaton rivers. It is a panorama of cropland, pastures, old fields, and grain- and livestock-farming areas.

The foundation of the region is 80 to 100 percent layers of sand-stone, thin limestone, and shale mixed with layers of coal and clay, which do not support the development of caves. The only cave-related features of this area are sandstone shelter and talus caves in a belt of land five to ten miles wide. Little in the way of artificial light is needed to explore them because they penetrate the bedrock less than seventy-five feet. The shelter caves are simply deep overhangs, and the talus caves are crevices in rock and boulder piles.

The most outstanding shelter caves are Morris Cave, with an entrance 151 feet wide and 25 feet high; Indian Shelter Cave, with an opening 101 feet wide and 20 feet high; and Jimmy-Jim Cave, with an entrance 200 feet wide and 25 feet high.

The caves of this area do not contain typical cave formations but they do feature gypsum flowers, ornate cross-bedding, and outstanding natural fretwork structures, which have the appearance of honeycomb or brickwork.

Springfield Cave Region

The eleven Missouri counties that constitute the Springfield Cave Region cover 6,633 square miles. A total of 1,457 caves were recorded here as of April 2007. The cave count, by county, is Barry, 144; Cedar, 19; Christian, 224; Dade, 55; Dallas, 27; Greene, 368; Lawrence, 44; Polk, 38; Stone, 305; Taney, 149; and Webster, 84.

This scenic Ozark region is home to Springfield, the largest city in the Ozarks, and Branson, the "Country Music Capital of the Ozarks." Vacationers also flock to one of the nation's oldest theme parks, Silver Dollar City, to Lake Taneycomo, a trout fisherman's paradise, and to Table Rock Lake, one of Missouri's largest man-made recreational reservoirs.

Tourism is an old industry here and leads the economy. Where tourists congregated, show caves multiplied. Some of the caves that were used as show caves in this region are Civil War Cave (Smallin Cave), Crystal Cave (Jenkins Cave), Crystal Caverns, Doling Park Cave, Emerald Lake Cave (Martin Cave), Fantastic Caverns (Temple Caverns), Marvel Cave (Marble Cave), Old Spanish Cave, Sequiota Cave, Talking Rocks Cavern (Fairy Cave) and Wonder Cave. Four of these caves are still shown to the public.

Wild caves are everywhere in these hills. They are huge, lengthy, multilevel, and spectacular. At least a dozen caves have more than one mile of surveyed passage, and many of the remaining caves in the area are about a half-mile to a mile long.

Deep pit caves lurk in the hills, especially in Barry County, where Farwell Cave reaches a total depth of 227 feet. Two vertical drops in Brock Cave total 140 feet. The Devil's Hole plunges to 185 feet, and other pits in the region reach depths of 70 to 100 feet.

While endangered gray and Indiana bats use at least fifteen caves in the region for maternity sites and hibernating, it is the presence of the blind salamander, blind crayfish, and especially the Ozark cavefish that excites biologists about the underground resources of this area. The Ozark Cavefish National Wildlife Refuge has been established here in hopes of protecting these delicate creatures. The Ozark cavefish lives in only a few caves in southwestern Missouri, northwestern Arkansas, and northeastern Oklahoma. Another rare species is the Tumbling Creek snail, which lives in Tumbling Creek Cave, home of the Ozark Underground Laboratory near Protem in Taney County. This lab is the only underground cave laboratory in the United States.

Early in settlement history, saltpeter was mined from caves in the Springfield Cave Region. Moonshiners hid their brew in the caves during Prohibition, and guano miners and buried-treasure hunters stalked these caves as well.

Beauty reigns in these caves as the presence of so many show caves testifies, but wild caves harbor splendor as well. Gypsum needles and petals, cave pearls, giant rimstone dams, stalactites, stalagmites, drapery, and massive cascades of flowstone add to the features that attract spelunkers to these caves.

Two particular caves that grace this wonderful cave region must be mentioned. Both are time vaults—River Bluff Cave in Springfield in Greene County (described in Chapter 1), and Lon Odell Memorial Cave in Dade County. Lon Odell Memorial Cave, named for a pioneer caver of the region, preserves ancient Native American footprints, "stoke" marks (where an Indian who explored the cave had rubbed torch bundles to keep his fire burning), and the tracks of ancient cougar and bear.

St. Louis Cave Region

The three Missouri counties and one metropolitan area that constitute the St. Louis Cave Region cover 1,720 square miles. A total of 346 caves were recorded here as of April 2007. The cave count, by metropolitan area and county areas, is City of St. Louis, 29; counties of Jefferson, 162; St. Charles, 22; and St. Louis, 133. Most of the notable caves are located in Jefferson and St. Louis counties. St. Charles County and the City of St. Louis have very few caves listed.

One of the characteristics that distinguish the caves in the St. Louis region is their vertical development along fissures in the bedrock. Pit-entry caves are fairly common. Several pits drop 60 to 70 feet. Breezy Pit plunges to a depth of 106 feet. Crescent Pit reaches a depth of 120 feet; it is the deepest pit cave in the St. Louis area, and it also features a high waterfall.

Lengthy caves are not uncommon here. Cave of the Falls is the area's longest cave with 2.8 miles of surveyed passage, and Catacomb Cave has more than one mile of passage.

Overhang Cave in St. Louis County has yielded the bones of a bear. Gray bats frequent Pleasant Valley Cave, which is one of the better-known wild caves in the area. And one cave in the area was completely destroyed by onyx miners about 1900.

Parks and special areas noted for their caves include Castlewood State Park, Cliff Cave Park, Bohrer Park, and Rockwoods Reservation.

The most important phase in the history of the caves of the St. Louis area was their use by breweries during the nineteenth century. One of these was Cherokee Cave, formerly used by the Lemp Brewery and noted for its ice age animal fossils. It was also a popular show cave in the 1950s.

FOR MORE READING

S ome of the books and periodicals listed below are out-of-print, and copies are scarce. Several of them can be examined in the Missouri Center for the Book Collection, Missouri State Library, 600 West Main, PO Box 387, Jefferson City, MO 65102-0387.

Adventures at Mark Twain Cave, by H. Dwight Weaver with illustrations by Paul A. Johnson (Jefferson City: Discovery Enterprises, 4th printing, 1977). This book explores the history of Mark Twain Cave from its discovery in 1819 to the 1960s. (Out of print.)

Adventures Underground in the Caves of Missouri, by Hazel Rowena Powell (New York: Pageant Press, 1953). This book contains brief descriptions of fourteen show caves open to the public in Missouri in the early 1950s. (Out of print.)

Cave Regions of the Ozarks and Black Hills, by Luella Agnes Owen (New York: Johnson Reprint, 1970). This is a reprint of Luella Owen's classic book published in 1898, the first book to focus attention on the geology of Missouri caves.

Caves of Missouri, by J Harlen Bretz (Rolla: Missouri Geological Survey and Water Resources, 1956). This book explains Bretz's theory for the origin of caves in Missouri, provides geological evaluations on caves with provisions for visitors, and gives a county-by-county summary of cave information and geological observations by Bretz. (Out of print.)

Exploring Missouri Caves: A Guidebook for the 1997 Convention of the National Speleological Society, edited by Robert L. Taylor and Jonathan B. Beard (Huntsville, Ala.: National Speleological Society, 1997). This book is an excellent reference on caves in the Meramec River basin area.

Geologic Wonders and Curiosities of Missouri, by Thomas R. Beveridge (2d ed., revised by Jerry D. Vineyard; Rolla: Missouri Department of Natural Resources, Division of Geology and Land Survey, 1990). This is an informative and entertaining book with much cave-related information.

Indians and Archaeology of Missouri, by Carl H. Chapman and Eleanor F. Chapman (Columbia: University of Missouri Press, 1964). This is an excellent early study of the archaeology of Missouri.

Lost Caves of St. Louis, by Hubert Rother and Charlotte Rother (St. Louis: Virginia Publishing, 1996). This book contains maps, photos, and historical information on a selection of old brewery caves beneath the city streets of St. Louis.

MCKC Digest. This quarterly periodical was published by the Missouri Caves and Karst Conservancy (MCKC) from 1995 to 2002 and contains many interesting articles about Missouri caves and cave conservation, management, and preservation.

Meramec Caverns in Legend and History, by H. Dwight Weaver with illustrations by Paul A. Johnson (Jefferson City, Mo.: Weaver and Johnson, 2d ed., 1995). This book gives a complete history of Meramec Caverns from its discovery in the 1720s to the present day. Available at Meramec Caverns.

Missouri Conservationist 61, no. 3 (March 2000). This was a special issue of the magazine on Missouri caves. Subjects include karst, groundwater, cave life, bats, and cave history.

Missouri Geology: Three Billion Years of Volcanoes, Seas, Sediments, and Erosion, by A. G. Unklesbay and Jerry D. Vineyard (Columbia: University of Missouri Press, 1992). An excellent layman's guide to the geology of Missouri and the origin of Missouri caves.

Missouri's Ice Age Animals, by M. G. Mehl (Rolla: Department of Business and Administration, Division of Geology Survey and Water Resources, 1962). This is the first book to be published on the ice age animals of Missouri. It is still an excellent primer.

Missouri Speleology. Published by the Missouri Speleological Survey, Inc., this is a quarterly journal that features cave maps and descriptions, as well as papers devoted to the many disciplines that characterize cave data collection and research in Missouri. Many issues provide cave information for a particular county.

Missouri: The Cave State, by H. Dwight Weaver with illustrations by Paul A. Johnson (Jefferson City: Discovery Enterprises, 1980). This book covers the romance of Missouri cave history, explores the cave regions of Missouri in depth, features information about Missouri cavers and caving, and contains appendices with statistical information. (Out of print.)

Onondaga: The Mammoth Cave of Missouri, by H. Dwight Weaver with illustrations by Paul A. Johnson (Jefferson City: Discovery Enterprises, 1973). This book is a complete history of the discovery, exploration, and development of Onondaga Cave at Onondaga Cave State Park. (Out of print.)

Paradigms of the Past: The Story of Missouri Archaeology, by Michael J. O'Brien (Columbia: University of Missouri Press, 1996). This book provides an in-depth look at the history of archaeology in Missouri and how the views of archaeologists have changed through time.

The Petroglyphs and Pictographs of Missouri, by Carol Diaz-Granados and James R. Duncan (Tuscaloosa: University of Alabama Press, 2000). This book documents Missouri's rich array of petroglyphs and pictographs, analyzing the many aspects of these rock carvings and paintings to show how such representations of ritual activities can enhance our understanding of Native American culture.

Springs of Missouri, by Jerry D. Vineyard and Gerald L. Feder (Rolla: Missouri Department of Natural Resources, Division of Geology and Land Survey, 1982). This book contains much information on the springs and spring caves of the Missouri Ozarks.

The Wilderness Underground: Caves of the Ozarks Plateau, by H. Dwight Weaver; James N. Huckins and Rickard L. Walk, photo editors (Columbia: University of Missouri Press, 1992). This is a one-of-a-kind book on caves of the Ozark region. It features many award-winning full-color cave photos, and the text provides an overview on many topics about caves in the Ozark region of Missouri and Arkansas.

World Wide Web sites. A great deal of useful information about Missouri caves and caving groups can be found on the Internet. First, check out mospeleo.org, then use the search words "Missouri caves." It takes only a few minutes of viewing Web sites to find links for all of the show caves and caving groups in Missouri.

INDEX

ABOUT THE AUTHOR

Former show cave operator H. Dwight Weaver is
the author of nine books, including *Wilderness
Underground: Caves of the Ozark Plateau,* also published by the University of Missouri Press, and
most recently *History and Geography of Lake of the
Ozarks.* He lives near Eldon, Missouri.